The characters and events portrayed in this boo from the ones who aren't. Any similarity to real pe ving or dead, is coincidental and not intended by the author, especially if they are litigious.

First published in 2020

Cover design by: Jodie Herron

This book is dedicated to all the lovely people in my life – you know who you are.

Crackwillow
Press

Table of Contents

[CHAPTER 1] — INTRODUCTION

As a first-time author, there's nothing more intimidating than the first line. Well, with that hurdle admirably cleared, I shall begin. At the time of writing, I'm a 58-year-old man who, amongst other things, has been playing the bass guitar in cover bands for most of my life. This spectacular career, well, successful-ish career......okay, long career has given me a great deal of pleasure and an awful lot of laughs and funny moments which I've been threatening to commit to paper for many a year, mainly to share these moments with anyone that cares to read this book, and to put a smile on their face. It certainly hasn't been for the money, that's for sure.

I've also amassed a reasonable amount of knowledge on the subjects of bass guitars, equipment, bands, gigs, musicians and all that goes with this peculiar but rewarding hobby, that I'd like to share. Some of it may be of use to the reader, but hopefully it will mainly be entertaining. Anecdotes? Oh yes, there's plenty of them. Some names may have been changed to protect the culprits (and my hide), but it is only right and proper that they get an airing to a greater audience than those who were there at the time.

I thought that the best format for this book would be to kick off with an autobiography, as that appears to be the format that big time musicians use to explain (justify?) what got them to where they are now, or in my case, didn't get me anywhere notable. Still, it made me happy. This will then be followed up with various themed sections on equipment, auditions, rehearsals etc., which will enable me to share some of the advice, knowledge and mistakes both acquired and endured over the years. I'd like this book to be half biographical, half advisory, and half testimony to my appalling grasp of maths.

Why now? Well, it's quite simple. It's March 2020, and we're in the midst of the Coronavirus pandemic. My wife and I bought a Bed and Breakfast business in the village of Dunster in Somerset almost one year ago, and it was going really well. However, we now have no guests, most incoming comms are people cancelling, the village is deserted, the supermarkets are depleted by panic-buying fuckwits dressed like members of Jesse James' Hole In The Wall gang, and we have to socially distance ourselves by at least two metres from everybody else. It looks like we're living off full English breakfasts for the foreseeable future.

We can't visit our elderly relatives, pregnant relatives, or indeed any relatives or friends - government advice to stop the virus spreading. They have closed cinemas, restaurants, cafes, gyms, tea rooms, major shops, minor shops and bars and pubs. As one internet wit pointed out "I can remember when we could smoke in pubs, now we can't even fucking drink in them!"

Having watched The Shining and Jack Nicholson's isolated demise from budding author to psychopathic maniac intent on killing his family with an axe, I'm aware of the risks but feel confident that it won't happen to me.

Edit: I've just deleted the penultimate chapter entitled "All work and no play makes Jack a dull boy" as it was very 'samey', said my rather worried looking wife.

The village of Dunster is fundamentally a medieval village with roads originally designed around the horse and cart transport system, and car parking has long been an issue. Not any more, folks. I was almost inspired to take a photo of four empty consecutive car park spaces in the village midday yesterday. It has suddenly got very serious.

So, having busied ourselves with what we could, which even included cleaning the radiators (yup, that bored) and being upset to find that the log fire didn't need making up today (damn, that would have occupied ten minutes), I thought I'd kick off this long overdue narrative of my life and musical career. There's no gigs to play at, no rehearsals, no auditions to prepare for, no songs to learn for a first dance at a wedding and there may be no bugger left alive to actually buy and enjoy this book, but hey ho, onwards and upwards.......

Legal notice: Any similarity between any characters in this book, and anyone dead or not dead, may be entirely circumstantial, or it may not be. Any offence caused probably wasn't intended except for a few, who've had it coming for a long time. Should you be one of these offended folk, write your own book and get your own back, it's a free world.

[CHAPTER 2] — EARLY YEARS

I was born in a nursing home on the 26th of February 1962, the first of three boys for my parents Peter and Sheila. I never did establish if they repeated the exercise to try and get things right. Although I have no recollection of the event, the nursing home was in sight of the River Tyne in Newcastle, which makes me a Geordie by birth, although the accent left me behind many years ago. Had the criteria been within smell of the River Tyne, I'm assured half the new-borns at that time could also claim to be Geordies.

My parents had originally met at work, at the Queen's cinema just off Northumberland Street in central Newcastle; my father was a projectionist and my mother was an usherette. The cinema was undoubtedly the source of my parents' love for music. My mother loved the big musical films (The King And I,

The Sound Of Music, amongst others) whereas my father adored cinema organ music (Wurlitzers, Reg Dixon and a weekly radio show called The Organist Entertains, which I'm surprised was even allowed – innocent times, eh?)

I grew up, with these dubious musical foundations, in a village called Carville, close to the city of Durham. The city is steeped in history with some spectacular bridges and buildings, chiefly the castle and cathedral, all of which was wasted on me. The cathedral served only to launch our woodwork project balsa wood aeroplanes over the city from the top of the main tower, and the bridges were for walking along on top of the stone side railings on the way home from school, an activity that could, with the benefit of hindsight, be termed 'cheating death'.

Belmont Primary School, my first school, was dull, and the introduction of recorder lessons did nothing to help the situation. The recorder must be the most unmusical whining instrument ever invented, and perfect pitch with a recorder can only be achieved if you throw it in a rubbish skip without it touching the sides. Three Blind Mice? Well, they could still hear the damn recorder even if they could not see it.

Whinney Hill Grammar School was next and was brutal. The proximity to Durham Maximum Security Prison was a great concern to our parents, but a source of hope for us pupils. If only they would escape and take us hostage, and then we'd skip double French with the formidable Mrs Dawson, whose first name was Vera. Her initials on my annual report were, and still are, a source of great pleasure. However, she thought my handwriting and that of David Jupp's was appalling so we were caned twice, on each hand. I never did work out how rendering a child's hand to be swollen, throbbing and unusable would improve their handwriting, but hey, teachers knew best in those days.

For geography homework I once had to write up which rivers and seas ships would cross to get from A to B, B being a random English port. I naively thought the Bristol Channel and the English Channel were one and the same, hence had every ship sailing up the Bristol Channel, to err, Hull or Dover. Result? Nope, not total gridlock at Bristol Docks, instead another caning. I wasn't joking when I said brutal.

Music lessons were both humorous and dreadful, with the weakest teacher in the school, one Miss Crawford. We sought vengeance for the acts of brutality inflicted by the other teachers on us, and the ever-tearful Miss Crawford was seen to be fair game. We all sat musical aural tests and those of us that passed qualified for violin lessons. Once we'd worked out that we'd have to cart yet another bag or case on two bus rides and a long walk, and we'd actually heard what a violin sounded like, we quickly declined.

We chose instead to see how quickly we could reduce Miss Crawford, or 'Crogger' to tears (again). One tried and tested method was when she introduced us to musical rounds. The boys had to sing "Bop bop showaddywaddy" while the girls took the far more complex lead vocals. We enjoyed it so much that we carried on and on, even when the girls stopped singing, Crogger stopped playing the piano, Crogger started shouting at us to stop, and Crogger stormed out of the classroom to get the headmaster, still with the entire class 1A male voice choir singing "Bop bop showaddywaddy" as she went. It probably resulted in yet another caning, albeit an almost deserved one for once.

At some point in these years, along came music. Proper music. Us eleven-year-old youngsters noticed that the bigger boys had ornate band names and logos painted on their haversacks (far cooler than the briefcases we quickly abandoned). They also had record albums under their arms when they waited for the bus home at Durham bus station. These albums seemed to be either by Yes or Pink Floyd, and we quickly made the correlation between bigger, older, more mature, cooler, and record albums. Thus, it began.

[CHAPTER 3] — FORMATIVE STUFF

At some point I was given a record voucher as a Christmas present and to my eternal shame the first single I bought was “Ernie, The Fastest Milkman In The West”, by Bennie Hill. This was quickly followed by a Top Of The Pops album (resplendent with tank topped dolly bird on the cover) with hits of the moment, performed by 'similar artists' in very small print. Dissimilar, more like - Blockbuster by The Sweet even had a different siren at the start.

My first proper band was The Sweet, and my bedroom became a shrine to them. I bought second-hand cassettes by The Sweet from Durham Indoor Market when possible and loved the look of horror on my parents' faces when they performed on Top Of The Pops. Watching The Sweet top the charts with Blockbuster with Steve Priest, their bassist, wearing a spiked World War 1 German helmet was just divine, as was their reaction to Roy Wood from Wizard singing See My Baby Jive. See My Parents Wince, more like.

As well as Top Of The Pops, I also listened to Radio 1, Radio Luxembourg and Metro Radio, a Newcastle-based FM station; all of these were a steady source of the music that was becoming ever more important to me. These were innocent times, and little did I know that a Radio Times magazine from this era would eventually become a sex offenders' register.

Then along came The Quo. Or rather, then we took notice of them - haven't they always been around? Songs like Down Down, Paper Plane and Caroline, and especially the look, had us snared. My friends and I quickly became walking denim mannequins. Forget the modern sin of double denim, this was quadruple denim (shirt, waistcoat, jacket and jeans) by Levi ideally, Wrangler occasionally, and Lee or Brutus if you were weird or unfortunate respectively. It was somewhat of a blessing to both our feet and genitals that you couldn't get denim socks or underwear. There was even Denim aftershave, to compensate for this shortfall, presumably with that distinctive aroma of err, old jeans??

My first proper album was The Story Of The Who by (oh, work it out) and singles wise I believe was Bohemian Rhapsody by Queen, I much preferred the B side, “I'm In Love With My Car”, and my youngest brother still has this single in his possession for 'safe keeping' and won't give it back. His denial of Freddie Mercury being gay, at a time when it was definitely uncool to be gay, was admirable if somewhat futile, and something I will share with the rest of the watch at his fire station one day.

The record album collection kept growing. Quo by (another toughie to work out), along with Sabotage by Black Sabbath, The Song Remains The Same by Led Zeppelin and A Night At The Opera by Queen being notable highlights, and still firm favourites to this day. Dark Side Of The Moon by Pink Floyd was acquired, complete with several free posters included. One of these was a shot of the Pyramids with a blue filter, and it was the done thing to stick this on the bedroom wall upside down, to confuse the parents. I didn't understand it then or now, but I still did it.

My father had a very expensive stereo system (much to my mother's chagrin) which was normally kept busy with Reg Dixon's Cinema Organ Greats and the like, and rarely a Howard Keel album to placate my mother. He once sullied the stylus with Dark Side Of The Moon while I watched, and I thoroughly enjoyed his amazement at The Floyd's use of stereo with bizarre sounds going from speaker to speaker. The music itself still left him cold, and Reg Dixon soon regained his right and proper place on the turntable.

One notable mistake by a friend at the time was a purchase of a double live album by Tangerine Dream which was quickly lent to all and sundry and we concluded that it sounded like someone randomly leaning on a keyboard with a pot of boiling fat on a stove in the background. We were never going to be music critics for The Guardian, but at least we were honest.

[CHAPTER 4] – MOVING SAARF

At some point in April 1976 we moved from Durham to Thame, near Oxford. New friends, new school (comprehensives were a lot less brutal than grammar schools, with almost optional attendance) and new music. Speech wise, they all sounded like country bumpkins whereas I was apparently borderline indecipherable. My classmates even created a Geordie to English dictionary, to help the situation.

With the new music came Nazareth, The Scorpions, Cheap Trick, UFO, Genesis, Dr Feelgood, John Otway (local musician/lunatic) and Motörhead. There was also Blondie, and Debbie Harry helped many of us teenage males get a really good *ahem* grip on things.

My first gig was Overdose, a school band, one evening in the school assembly hall. We had no tickets, so forced an entry via the school kitchens, where my mother used to work (I hope she never reads this). The band were really good and featured a guest spot from a friend of mine on lead air guitar, mainly because he had long hair. We later shared a joint outside with the head prefect. All in all, a very good night. I was warming to the comprehensive scholastic system.

My first proper gig was seeing Nazareth at the Hammersmith Odeon in London, and that was just awesome. They were a cracking band, with lots of great catchy rock songs in their set. They even had a break in the middle when four chairs were put on the stage, and they did three or four songs acoustically. This was well before unplugged had been invented. I can remember it all vividly, and thought I'd love to play in a band one day.

Then along came Punk and particularly The Jam, The Clash, The Sex Pistols, The Damned, The Buzzcocks and The Stranglers. Primarily brash, angry, aggressive (and often intelligent) songs that were bursting with energy, and everything pretty much changed for me, musically. The Annie Nightingale Sunday night radio show became the source for most new tunes, as many of the mainstay radio DJ stalwarts didn't quite know what to make of the music. John Peel was another notable exception.

I remember queuing up outside the local record shop in Thame waiting for it to open, to purchase Never Mind The Bollocks, Here's The Sex Pistols on its release day (the posters in the window had the offending 'B' word covered by black tape. Said record shop had saved the day in earlier times when my parents went to buy Strangers In The Night, a live double album by UFO, as a birthday present for me. They remembered the title, but not the band, and apparently, I had a close escape from one of Frank Sinatra's long players.

Two school friends took a picture of The Jam to the barbers and asked for a haircut like Paul Weller's. They emerged with number two grade skinhead haircuts. "Paul Weller doesn't have his hair cut like this" - "He would if he came here and I did it" is a conversation that didn't happen, but really should have.

Two other friends dyed their hair jet black and became Thame's Black Haired Punks. BHP graffiti frequently appeared around the Thame area, but the local CID never did manage to work out the culprits. They can't have tried too hard to crack that case.

It was around this time that the New Wave Of British Heavy Metal also came along, and provided us with the likes of Saxon, Def Leppard, Diamondhead, Iron Maiden (when they had a singer, not a screamer), Judas Priest (who always had a screamer for a singer), Samson, who had a screamer for a singer who left and went on to scream for Iron Maiden)

Aylesbury Civic Centre had an internal bar and stage which became the “Friar’s Club” on a Friday and Saturday night. You had to be a member to get in and buy a ticket, but as we frequently lost our membership cards, we just re-joined again and again. For a small club they had some awesome bands on, including Dr Feelgood, The Clash, The Police, Gary Numan, Genesis, Marillion, Kajagoogoo and The Jam. A friend still has a paper pasty dish signed by Bruce Foxton from The Jam, and it is to my eternal regret that I missed that gig.

I didn't miss the gig by Ken Liversausage and the Vice Creams, which culminated in two balloon topped penal effigies either side of the stage being burst by two scantily clad girls, only to discover the balloons were full of shaving foam which sprayed across the front rows of the audience. Happy days.

It was at this point that I decided that I really wanted to play guitar and be in a band. Not the exact Ken Liversausage climactic point, but there or thereabouts - I have some pride. However, the whole activity had to be put on hold for want of a guitar and amp, but primarily a guitar teacher, of which there was a distinct lack of, in our little Oxfordshire market town of Thame.

[CHAPTER 5] – HELLO, I'M HHHHHHAIRO

About a year later, I had a job in the local mass production pizza factory, King Harry Foods in Thame (I'd go back tomorrow if it still existed). It was mainly staffed by Rover workers from Cowley who took redundancy (and a great many spare parts for their Minis, Marinas and Allegros) and transferred their automotive skills to helping to make one million frozen pizzas a week. It was a seamless transition, which might suggest just why Rover failed. The frequent redeployment of alternators, brakes, steering racks, and exhaust systems to their employees' home garages, and the night shift generally being paid to sleep in the air conditioning ducting may also have played a part.

Still, I had a job, money and a car, so I contacted the man behind the recently advertised Guitar Lessons ad in the Thame Gazette, one Jairo Zaldua. The 'J' in Jairo is silent and is replaced by a great many 'H's - it's a Spanish thing. He lived in a nearby village but taught from a studio at his sister-in-law's house (for studio read spare bedroom). When we met, and he'd finished pronouncing all the 'H's that his name didn't have, he asked me why I wanted to learn to play guitar. My answer was to be in a band (I didn't mention girls, money, fame and all that went with it, but I was certainly thinking it). He declared that he only taught classical guitar, but if you can play that, you can play anything (with a great deal more unnecessary 'H's).

Suitably convinced, and with no other option really, I signed up and bought a classical guitar and case. One lesson a week, for one hour, at £5. Payment was also possible in boxes of frozen 'reject' pizzas, which were neither rejects nor even paid for by yours truly - I was adapting to the Rover worker philosophy. The more boxes the merrier he said, until the Saturday morning I arrived with my Mini packed with about twenty boxes and caused chaos with his entire extended family's frozen food storage facilities. He must have been forgiven, as I believe he eventually left his wife and moved in with his sister-in-law. They probably bonded during Pizzagate.

Lessons progressed quite well with me mastering such classics as Etude in G Major - I'm guessing all the Etudes in the other keys were just crap, and never caught on. There was also Greensleeves, the theme from Love Story, the theme from The Alamo and many more themes, not one of which I've ever had requested at a gig. But if they did, I'd be ready....... I think I got to a point whereby I could almost get through Cavatina without too many errors, thus leaving John Williams unthreatened.

Following a job change to a transformer manufacturing company (electrical transformers, not the toys) I started going to college one day a week in Oxford and had a life defining conversation with a college mate who played guitar.

Gavin: "Why are you learning classical guitar?"
Me: "I want to be in a band."
Gavin: "Why don't you just buy a bass instead?"
Me: "Ohhhh....." (Ding - lightbulb moment)

Fast forward to an Oxford music shop, and the purchase, with Gavin's assistance, of a Vox something or other natural finish bass guitar, and a small practice combo. My first bass......but not the last, by a long way. Next stop was Gavin's house with me playing the bass line of Fleetwood Mac's Albatross (two notes, as I recall, with the odd tricky change from one to the other) while Gavin laid down the lead guitar line perfectly on his Strat.

This ignited a voracious appetite for books on bass and playalong tuition tapes. Having mastered You're So Vain, Ghostbusters, Rock Around The Clock and The Kids In America playalongs, the next step was to join a band.

Incidentally, and still music related, while working at the transformer company, the foreman took on a private job to build a very big, heavy (three-man lift) and totally bespoke electrical transformer for Radio Laser, a North Sea pirate radio station. Private in that he bought all the parts, and did all the winding, soldering and laminating after hours, and sold it for a very healthy profit. They wanted another one, and the general manager said, "I'll have some of that, this one's mine" and promptly stole the job from the foreman. He repeated the process, and expense, and labour, and the day before he was due to deliver it (and get paid), Radio Laser sank to the bottom of the North Sea. Karma.

[CHAPTER 6] – THE MAXIMUM VOLUME BAND

Following another job move, this time to a computer repair company back in Thame, there was an early days chat with my supervisor about hobbies. "Guitar, eh? That long-haired hippy git on the bench opposite plays guitar as well; you should talk to him". So, I did and it transpired that he'd just been sacked from the Ken Tomey Band. Given that his name was Ken Tomey, that's about as harsh as it gets. This was the same Ken Tomey Band that had topped the legendary Aylesbury Friar's Club annual poll of best bands the year before, beating John Otway, Marillion, The Clash and The Jam, to name just a few notable scalps.

> Me: "How on earth did you manage that?"
> Hippy: "Oh, we just pinched all the voting slips and filled them in ourselves, for our band."

(I told this story to John Otway's current lead guitarist at a gig only two years ago. He said "Otway will love that when I tell him, and probably wish he'd thought of it first")

That long haired git (Ken to his parents, Jesus to my children (there's a remote likeness), and Hippy to everyone else) told me that the guy on yet another bench with a big nose (the bloke, not the bench) played drums. Paul was his name, but he was always called Snod.

Which just left the vacancy for a singer. Guess what? That young skinny guy with the big gob and bad hair (aka Dennis, which became Den, which became Dendruff when we noticed a particular scalp condition, and then just Druff) on the front bench fancies having a go at being a singer.

Band sorted, we are up and running. Myself, Hippy, Snod and Druff had formed The Maximum Volume Band, or MVB for short, as we called ourselves. At a future 'trying to get a gig in a pub' meeting, the landlord sought reassurance that we weren't too loud, then asked what MVB stood for. Mainly Virginal Band was the answer, given that two members (ooh err) were still untouched by female hands. Needless to say, Snod and Druff (said virgins) were not present when we explained this to the landlord. "Hmm, odd name" he said. Still, we got the gig.

Hippy had a flare for writing good original riff-based rock songs aptly called Black Widow, Open Mind and Nightmare Zone to name but a few. He even churned out a tribute to our employers, Universal Computers Limited, called UCL Blues, mainly about the poor pay and prospects therein. We rehearsed at a succession of local village halls until we were invariably banned for being too loud and had to find the next willing victim/venue. We were lucky to find one isolated village hall on a hilltop, so volume wasn't a problem. Sorted, we thought, until winter came and we discovered there was no heating in the hall. Triplets were quickly mastered, mainly by syncopated shivering.

During one early rehearsal Druff was using a guitar amp as his vocal PA (proper gear came later) when a valve popped, and slightly scorched the valve holder in its death throes. Druff replaced the valve, but not before cleaning the valve holder with WD40 and leaving a small reservoir of the fluid sitting inside the holder. New valve inserted, power up and it started to glow. Result, thought Druff as he stood in front of the amp while we observed from the rear. "One two one two" was amplified perfectly through the amp and speaker. Job done we thought, but just to add some comedic value to the exercise Druff then shouted "Bang!" as loud as he could and started laughing as we winced.

We then too started to laugh, as the 'bang' had caused a surge in current which ignited the WD40 left in the valve holder and a small and rapidly spreading internal amp fire was under way. He laughed, we really laughed and pointed, he kept laughing with the occasional "What? What is it?" thrown in, until he too noticed the smoke and flames, and fatal demise of his amp, which did manage to amplify his "Fuuuuuuuuuuck!!!" before it finally passed away.

We eventually struck upon Waddesdon Village Hall, an imposing gothic style building in a village near Aylesbury. This had a stage, a small lighting rig, a sound limiter power trip that fortunately didn't work, and heating. Further classic songs that are still to be discovered were written, mastered and perfected here, such as Speedo Greebo, Bone Structure, The Globe, Come By, and The 5mm Thrust Song (don't ask). Following the attempted suicide of a works store man who was spurned by the works receptionist, our sympathy extended to writing a song called Overdose (opening line "I never thought much about my life, what was wrong and what was right"). Pure poetry.

Our first gig was at Thame Sports And Arts Centre as the opening band on a four band bill, for a Valentine’s Day Massacre musical extravaganza. The headline band were college kids with a big following, so we debuted to about 300 people. Overdose, Black Widow and The 5mm Thrust Song were politely received, and we were well pleased with ourselves.

More writing and rehearsing took place, and more gigs. The Cross Keys and Four Horseshoes in

Thame, The Common Rooms in Wheatley, The Buckingham Arms in Aylesbury were all quickly added to our list of conquered parishes.

The ubiquitous demo tape was the next stage for us, but on a minuscule budget. Gavin, my college friend, had a Tascam 4-track recorder and fortunately my folks were off on holiday leaving the house empty with the instructions to 'keep an eye on the place'. Better than that, I and four others took over the house for two days, cleared the dining room of all furniture, and created a recording studio of sorts. Borrowed microphones were taped to conveniently arranged items (otherwise known as my mother's finest chairs) and by the end of day one, we were ready to go.

Day two went well, with proper recording taking place. It was a hot day, so we opened the patio doors and myself and Hippy played our parts from the patio, no doubt much to the amusement of the old peoples' home opposite. Volume has high as was our way, but the house was detached and so no harm done, or so we thought. Druff thought he'd move to the patio too due to the heat to lay down some more vocals, only he used his amplified voice between songs to carry on an argument with the drummer, peppered with profanities aplenty. (Alliteration too – it's all in here)

I was in the middle of laying down another bass line from the patio when something caught my eye. I turned around to see two of Thames Valley Police's finest approaching, through my folk's garden.

> The Police: "Found you at last. We've had lots of complaints about the noise and language, and we've been trying to trace it for thirty minutes."
> Me: "If it took you thirty minutes to find us, we can't have been that loud."
> The Police: "Don't push it, or you're nicked. Stop it, now!"
> Me: "Okay, good point very well made, officer."

I did think to advise them that Druff was doing all the swearing, so they could arrest him if they wanted, but thought better of it. They left, the volume was turned down, we vacated the patio for the sweat box that was the dining room with all windows and doors closed, and what was to be entitled as The Pig Bust Jam was completed. I never did find out who had complained but was later reassured by a nurse at the old peoples' home opposite that the residents loved it.

The Pig Bust Jam was submitted to a friend who wrote a music column in the weekly Thame Gazette. All I can remember of the review was the headline "These Guys Are LOUD" which gave us an immense juvenile sense of pride, although ‘approved by local OAPs' never made it into the article.

Thame is remarkably close to Towersey, which holds an annual folk music festival, over several days, in August. In those days festivals really were as advertised (so no pop bands with one original member) and the UK's finest and mainly obscure folk bands performed to a field full of several thousand folk fans, none of whom looked out of place in a farmer's field.

Mainly due to Druff's ties with the organising committee (okay, he lived in Towersey), he was convinced he could get us on the bill albeit under false pretences, and a plan was hatched. The name (Maximum Volume Band) would give the game away, somewhat, so we toyed with rebranding as the Common Rural Agricultural Players (acronyms ruled, even then). We intended to take to the stage dressed in suitably attired farmer/folk wear, then as we launched into our opening song of Black Widow, rip off our smocks and wellies to reveal the mandatory denim, leather and the odd Jack Daniels t-shirt.

It never did happen (I'm not sure why, probably just apathy), and the prospect of achieving rock immortality as the first band to be pitchforked to death by screaming outraged folk fans wasn't achieved. In truth, the crowd would most likely have just clapped politely and drunk more cider, as was their wont, but we'll never know.

However, all was not well in the band, as Druff and Snod had a major fallout at most rehearsals, gigs and pretty much whenever they occupied the same space, culminating in the definitive argument as follows:

Snod: "You're a crap singer."
Druff: "You're an even crapper drummer."
Snod: "This is your first band, I've been in OTHER bands."
Druff: "Yup, CRAP bands."

It didn't augur well for the future, and I'm not sure who left first, but ultimately, they both did. Snod was replaced on drums by Dave, a lovely guy who's still jamming with Hippy to this day, and Druff was replaced by a succession of singers over time, all of whom left their mark, nay scars, on us.

[CHAPTER 7] – LINDEN AND DENZIL

Linden

The Maximum Volume Band went through several name changes, including Cemetery Junction, before we settled on England In Flames, for no good reason. We also had a succession of singers, the most memorable of which were Linden and Denzil, who brought to mind a pair of Cornish fishing villages, but weren't, sadly. That would have been preferable, in hindsight.

I believe Linden was the first singer after Druff. I use the term 'singer' loosely, because he couldn't really sing, but he could certainly perform. He was already a legend on the local karaoke scene where he was known as The Sheffield Viking resplendent with plastic horned helmet, peroxide blonde hair and a missing tooth, possibly for dramatic effect. He told us he wanted to front a proper rock band, and we fell for it. Various covers had crept into the set by now (Paranoid, Alright

Now, Rock and Roll, etc) partly at Linden's insistence, and all in preparation for a gig at the local top venue in Aylesbury, The Hop Pole pub. However, Linden had missed two rehearsals leading up to the gig but insisted the gig would go ahead and that he'd definitely make the rehearsal on the Tuesday before the gig on the Friday.

Come Tuesday, hall booked, three musos present, all gear loaded in and ready to go, but no Linden. We phoned him and he said that his car's engine had blown up and he couldn't make the rehearsal, but he'd be alright for the gig. We'd already noted, in the local newspaper, that there was a Karaoke competition final that very night in an Aylesbury pub, so we loaded the gear back into our cars, and headed for the very same pub.

Linden's distinctive Ford Escort was in the car park, parked neatly, with no visible signs of distress such as an oil leak - we did check. Inside the pub, lo and behold, was Linden. A rather sheepish Linden too, when he clocked us. He did apologise but then had to go and perform his song, as 'Elvis' had just finished.

He transformed into a budget version of Axl Rose complete with biker jacket and kilt, and rattled off a superb version of the Guns 'n' Roses classic Welcome To The Jungle....except for the singing, which was randomly on key, often off key, and generally a bit meh. However, he did swirl around, interact with the audience (except us), twirl the microphone stand around and delivered a first-class performance......bar the singing bit.

Shortly afterwards the results were announced, and Linden got first prize, which was a three-day luxury break in Singapore. How, we never quite worked out, and left feeling like we were the stupid ones, with a delighted Linden calling out "See you Friday night at The Hop Pole". Come Friday night at approximately 8:30pm I took a phone call at home from Linden at The Hop Pole.

> Linden: "Where are you? We're on in 30 minutes and all my mates are here."
> Me: "You're not going to believe this, but my car engine just blew up as well, so I can't make it to the gig."

Down went the phone. He got the same answer from the other two band members, Hippy and Dave, as pre-planned, on what was later to be referred to as 'The night Linden went solo'.

We may have missed our chance to gig at The Hop Pole, and we weren't going on a luxury mini break to Singapore, like some, but hey, at least we had our pride. Dave bumped into Linden some time afterwards, who humbly conceded "Fair enough, I had that coming."

Denzil

That was the end of Linden's time with the band, and we then recruited a guy called Denzil who, he proudly said, had been in loads of bands. All of them for not very long, we later found out. Denzil worked at the local psychiatric residential hospital and quite how he was allowed to walk out of there at the end of each workday was a mystery. He must have never been there during an audit, or we'd have lost him to the hospital completely.

Still, we always knew he'd be at a rehearsal because he couldn't drive, and one of us had to collect him, and take him back home afterwards. One infamous trip home with Hippy led to the following conversation:

> Denzil: "Could you drop me off in central Aylesbury, near the kebab van?"
> Hippy: "It's out of my way, but okay."
>
> They arrived at the van.
>
> Denzil: "Can you just wait here for a sec?"
> Hippy: "Okay."
> Denzil: "Oh, and can you lend me the money for a kebab, then run me home afterwards?"

Denzil was never short of confidence, nor cheek, but was always short of money. He could sing, although he leaned more towards a high-pitched Michael Jackson tone, complete with Jackson-esque vocal tics and squeals, rather than Ozzy or Robert Plant but we thought we'd try him for a while. Fundamentally, it was our band's turn to have him, or so it felt.

He wrote his own lyrics, and as we didn't have the hearing range of a canine, we often had no idea what he was singing about. Never more so than at a gig at The Nag's Head in High Wycombe, a particularly noteworthy venue that had seen many good bands play there over the years. And us.

Denzil: "This next song is for all the elephants in the world...take it away guys!!"

There was a collective WTF moment from us in the band, as we stared repeatedly at our set lists, not knowing what to play.

Me: "Elephants?? The next song is The Come By?"
Denzil: "That's the one, it's all about elephants."

Hence, we became much wiser that night. Well, about key elephant terms, any ways.

Denzil also had the annoying habit of facing you and kneeling down when he wasn't singing and shaking his head in a fervent manner directly in front of your crotch. Quite what it looked like to the audience I had no idea. Well, I did really, and that worried me. Particularly as Denzil was quite a 'sweaty' performer, so the crotch level head shaking was often accompanied by a random spray of brow sweat in all directions. I constantly thought; play the right notes, keep your head tilted back, don't open your mouth and try not to inhale. At least until he turns around and has to start singing again. Jeez, the things we do for our art.

For some bizarre reason we decided to book a recording studio in Bicester for four hours and commit our talent and four best songs to a properly recorded and mixed demo tape. We all played well as we laid down our respective tracks although when Hippy emerged from a booth having laid down his guitar solos, he did enquire as to the whereabouts of his Mars Bar.

Denzil: "Oh, I was hungry, so I ate it" which promptly cleared that little mystery up.

Cue Denzil's turn in the vocal booth to lay down some backing vocals, having already pronounced his skill and familiarisation with the recording process. Thirty seconds in, and I'm tapping on the window of the booth.

Me: "Your backing vocals are exactly the same as your 'fronting' vocals."

Denzil: "I know, but I want to give them some depth."
Me: "The engineer can do that with a button, you're supposed to do harmonies and 'Oh yeahs' and other stuff over the top, at the appropriate places....and stop fuckin' looking at my Mars Bar."
Denzil: "Oh okay, got it."

We ended up with four pretty decently recorded original rock songs, peppered with Michael Jackson on overdrive type tics, yelps and squeals throughout. And we had to pay his 25% of the cost as he had no money. And we had to give him a lift home. And hide any uneaten Mars Bars from him.

He was good at getting us gigs, only they weren't the venues that would ever receive us particularly well. Aylesbury Dry Ski Slope clubhouse springs to mind, where we were about as popular as a fart in a spacesuit. The Common Rooms in Wheatley was another such venue. The pub very reluctantly turned off the disco-laden jukebox as we started and launched into our hard rock set, and the audience just stood and glared at us. Third song in, and a punter approaches me, mid-song.

Punter: "Why don't you play some fuckin' disco songs?"
Me: "Er, we don't fuckin' know any, that's why."

Fifth song in, and the PA amp went up in smoke, sadly not taking Denzil with it. "Sorry guys, that's your lot for tonight" we said, and quietly thanked God for his timely intervention. As we were loading the gear out of the pub and back into the cars, we spotted Denzil at the bar trying to get us another booking at the same venue. He was quickly acquired by the throat, and he too was loaded back into a car, and we left there, also quickly, but at least intact.

He also had us booked into a pub in Croydon (a major drive away, but not for him) on a cold, wet Tuesday night in winter for some derisory amount like £75 in total, that we flatly refused to do.

I'm not quite sure why Denzil left the band. Any band member could have, and was entitled to, kill him, but didn't. He could have been force fed Mars Bars up to the point of asphyxiation, but wasn't, tempting though it was. He may even have been sectioned after an appraisal at work went wrong but whatever the true reason, he was gone. Thankfully.

[CHAPTER 8] – DECENT SINGERS

At some point thereafter, my first wife (at some point in the previous scribblings there had been a wedding, and two wonderful kids, Jodie and Liam were created – not during the wedding obviously, but some time afterwards) let it be known that two young kids and their demands were not compatible with band life, so I too stood down from the band. Rock and Roll by Zeppelin was replaced by Rock A Bye Baby by err, whoever. Bass guitars out, baby buggy in. Teething, crawling, walking, nappies, potty training and Walt Disney videos occupied all my free time, as it truthfully should.

About five years later I bumped into Dave, the drummer. "I wish you'd come back. Our current bassist is crap and very overweight and I'm sure the next time he has to carry his gear into the rehearsal hall, he'll just keel over and die – his face goes a very bright shade of red doing it now."

I mentioned the conversation to my first wife, who said why don't you give them a call and get involved again. Bugger! When did that light turn green, and I didn't notice? In fairness, the kids were older, and a bit easier by then, so I re-joined.

We recruited a great singer by the name of Rob, a lovely local guy who could sing and play guitar and was a pleasure to work with. A defining moment with Rob was when a neighbour of mine mentioned a charity bandathon that she was involved with to be held in Thame Town Hall. "There's all types of bands on, you'll fit right in and it's for a good cause too" was the successful pitch from her.

When we arrived before our allotted slot on the day we quickly found out that 'all types of bands' amounted to mainly brass bands, some woodwind bands, some swing bands, some big bands (think Glen Miller) and us, a hard rock originals and covers band. Rob announced us as "And now for something completely different...." And within five minutes the packed hall was cleared of virtually everybody, who prior to us had been enjoying The Thame Woodwind Quartet. Not only that, but our versions of Like A Hurricane and Paranoid were being piped outside via the PA, so we could gain yet further disproval from people who couldn't even see us to dislike us. In response to Rob's opening line, the brass band that followed us did open with a version of the Monty Python theme song. Touché, as they say.

Work wise I was now managing a team of engineers and one based in Croydon asked for a favour when part of his roof was removed in high winds on an especially busy day, and he needed time off.

> Me: "I thought you rented that flat? Isn't it the landlord's problem?"
> Engineer: "You don't understand. My ahem ‘attic plantation’ is now visible from the sky and if a police helicopter spots it, I'm in big trouble."

The short notice day off was granted, and duly rewarded when his weekly paperwork arrived at the office, complete with a small envelope of aromatic green leaves for me. Said leaves then reappeared at our next rehearsal, and about one third of them were rolled into a joint, which was then shared between us three smokers in the band (Hippy, the guitarist, always was Mr Squeaky Clean, so did not partake. Nothing happened at all, so a few songs later and another joint with another one third of the leaves. Still nothing. A few more songs, another joint using up the last of the 'gift', and still nothing. I was most perturbed, and pledged to give my 'dealer' from Croydon the worst jobs going at work for weeks on end.

Then it kicked in, and how. Hippy called out 'Paranoid' and launched into the opening riff, perfectly.

Dave, our drummer, suddenly couldn't hit a barn door with a guided missile, let alone something as tiny as a snare or kick drum pedal, and promptly fell off his drum stool, giggling as he went. Rob on vocals also resorted to manic giggling rather than: "Finished with my woman 'cos she couldn't help me with my mind etc."

Me? Well I thought I knew which strings to hit with a pick, only they'd turned into the longest, floppiest, most rubber-like strings I'd ever encountered. I too found this very funny and joined in with the giggling. Hippy was most put out to be surrounded by three hysterical gibbering wrecks for the rest of the rehearsal. My 'dealer' later told me to be careful with that stuff, it's a bit of a creeper. Too late, far too late.

With the rehearsal completed / abandoned (delete as per your perspective) it then dawned on three of us that we each had to drive home in our current conditions. We all managed it, but I believe adopted the same approach as me, which was to drive very, very carefully, and very, very slowly. I think 3mph was the average speed for me (I may have hit 4mph on a downhill slope, briefly), and I believe the other two followed suit.

Later that year we had a gig at The Aristocrat in Aylesbury, and it was going very well. Three attractive young ladies approached us at the start of the second set and asked us to open with “Knocking On Heaven's

Door". Always happy to oblige, we did, and promptly noticed a very tall biker dancing towards us with strange arm movements. It made sense when he finally reached us and started waving a bottle in each of our faces, and demanded we stop. Again, still happy to oblige, we stopped. Weren't we the most obliging band, ever?

"Nothing personal lads, but we don't want that song, in this pub, now. We have a mate in hospital after a bike crash, and things aren't good". It did seem rather personal to me, with a bottle waving about in front of my nostrils, but hey ho. The defence that 'the girls wanted that song' was never offered and would not have worked anyway.

We turned towards one another for an impromptu mid-gig crisis band meeting to discover our drummer was hastily packing down his kit. "I know him, he's hard as nails and nasty with it, and if he's in that sort of a mood he will kick off again, and I'm not going to be here when he does." Thank you and goodnight, Aristocrat regulars, we'll be back (a line later purloined and made famous by Arnie in The Terminator, for sure).

Rob was yet another singer who left, and I can't remember why. I know there was a bit of a scene with the neighbours who originally said they'd be okay with his son learning the drums at home, but who then served a noise abatement order on him after a matter of weeks. He probably moved away.

Rob was replaced by Tony, a good singer and rhythm guitarist, but who often had commitment issues. My favourite excuse of his was "The builders turned up three weeks early to deliver a pile of sand and left it in front of my garage door, so I can't get to any of my gear". Builders who were three weeks early? Yeah, right.

A few more singers followed, including one who clearly didn't like me and took it upon himself to mix down my bass lines on another demo tape to a level generally referred to as 'inaudible' and then claim that the engineer (a friend of his) had taped over the master tape. 'Tosser' sprung to mind, both then and now.

Everything came to a head when my marriage failed. I had a job move to Birmingham and started a new relationship up there, which quickly reached the status of co-habitation, and, despite commuted rehearsals for a while, I ultimately left my first band for good.

[CHAPTER 9] – HELLO BIRMINGHAM

I found Birmingham to be very different to Thame, certainly language wise. However, the live music scene was much better, as was the band scene, and I embarked on a series of generally bizarre auditions and band startups that invariably failed. Some of the more spectacular were as follows:

> Guitarist: "We've got full practice facilities in the singer's small factory, just bring your bass."
> Me: "Okay, see you Wednesday night."
>
> Guitarist, on Wednesday night: "Nice bass, where's your bass amp and speakers?"
> Me: "You said to just bring my bass, so I did."
> Guitarist: "Well I meant bass AND amp."
> Me: "Perhaps you should have said that, then."

Having managed to inadvertently create a very unpleasant atmosphere, I set about performing the audition songs well enough, despite getting my audible tone via a line in to a pretty poor PA. However, between every song, the guitarist was constantly fussing over the (female) singer's hair. It transpired he was a sales rep for Wella hair products, and a Wella rep never rests, or so it seemed. I gave that one a miss.

Then there was the police audition (rather than an audition for The Police, sadly). The initial phone conversation went well, and the audition itself had gone well. Afterwards, we paused for a chat and the question of our day jobs arose. It transpired that the singer, guitarist and drummer were all serving police officers.

> Me: "That's a coincidence, we're all kinda in the same industry."
> Them: "Are you in the force too?"
> Me: "No, I'm a drug dealer."

It was only meant as a joke but if ever a joke was to suffer a spectacular and immediate death, it was that one. I'm still waiting to hear if I got the gig or not. 'Not' is the hot favourite.

There followed an audition with a reasonable bunch of guys who could all play, bar the rhythm guitarist, who clearly couldn't. Every time he played an incorrect chord, he dived down to his pedal board and tweaked the same pedal, like it would help. I had to ask. "What else does that pedal do, apart from always generate the wrong chord?". Another band I never heard back from.

There was a Status Quo tribute band startup that went like a dream, and within three rehearsals we were up to about twenty songs. With Quo bass lines that's not too hard to achieve, although your right wrist is doing things it hasn't had to do since you were a teenager. Then we all got a text from 'Francis Rossi' who said he was packing it all in, just like that. That one was a shame.

There was a most interesting audition followed by a few months with a female fronted rock band. The singer's day job was working from a flat near Birmingham's Broad Street inflicting pain and suffering on a variety of well-heeled men (she though, had much higher, and far spikier heels) who paid for the privilege, which sometimes included a swift boot to their nether regions. Having experienced that physical sensation myself many years previously at a Karate lesson (I'd forgotten my protective box on that night) quite why someone would actually pay to experience it totally escaped me. She proudly boasted that while her day job was 'different' the redeeming feature was that "There's no sex, though". Phew, that's alright, then. Squeaky darn clean, almost.

This band also had a hanger on, who turned up for every rehearsal and whose sole purpose was to change the batteries in our in-ear monitoring packs, should they fail. Not exactly a career with prospects in the music industry, but he was happy, particularly when one of us needed batteries. The rehearsals went well, and the first gig was looming. However, prior to the last rehearsal my partner's mother was taken gravely ill and hospitalised.

I informed the band by text in between frequent visits to the Intensive Care Unit, only to receive a phone call whilst on the ward from the lead singer and semi-professional ball kicker herself. She told me I was fired, that I'd wasted all their time and that they'd had to cancel the gig. Slightly taken aback (!) I told her that I had the set nailed, was potentially good for the gig if things stabilised, but that really, some things were rather more important than a band and a gig. Evidently, they aren't, and I remained fired. I guess she enjoyed her work, and that I was lucky not to be charged for that virtual kick in the nads. A bullet dodged, was my conclusion. Also, bizarrely, I'm still friends with the battery monitor on Facebook.

There was one audition where the drummer played while leaning forward and just glaring at me for the whole audition, like I'd slept with his wife, set fire to his house and reversed over his dog. To the best of my knowledge I hadn't, but by the end of the night I almost felt like I ought to, unless his dog was particularly cute, and his wife particularly wasn't.

There was the Queen tribute startup band, and initially tales of gigs in Dubai that 'Freddie' was saying 'no' to, until the band was up and running. Thank heaven it never was, as I know the Dubai penal system is somewhat brutal and impersonating a popular band with a singer who kept going off key was probably punishable by 50 lashes and 5 years of hard labour. I'm sure that Dubai soap on a rope isn't the nicest, either.

Generally, when a singer misses a note, they are aware, and often apologise at the end of the song. Not 'Freddie'. He'd miss them by a metric mile, then say "That song's in the bag too, chaps". I have no idea just where this 'bag' is, and truly never want to find out. A lovely guy all the same, and a prime candidate for a before and after advert and sale, if anyone from Autotune is reading.

Still, it wasn't all bad, as the next chapters detail. Amidst this chaos there were some very good bands. Read on.....

[CHAPTER 10] – GINGER MULE

My first reasonably successful band in the Midlands was Ginger Mule, named after a winter cocktail on a beer mat in a pub during a 'We really need a name' crisis meeting. Different, obscure but most importantly, not taken by any other band. I found a thread on Basschat (the definitive UK forum for all things bass (no, not the fish)) about the most popular songs in your covers band's set and raided it to create the perfect set list, theoretically.

After a bit of advertising, auditioning and recruiting we were up and running. Or we were, until our singer sent us a text saying, "I quit, and please don't try to contact me, ever". I never did get to the bottom of that one. Well, I couldn't, because he said not to. Strange breed, singers.

More advertising and the drummer came to a singer-less rehearsal one night clutching a sheet of paper and saying that he'd knocked up an advert to be placed at rehearsal rooms and music shop notice boards, as was common in those days. Our keyboard player said I hope it's not one of those tacky ones with the silhouette of a singer in a band line up with a question mark over it, and the legend 'it could be you'. "Errrrr no", said the drummer, quietly crumpling up his bit of paper, stuffing it in his pocket and saying he'd bring it along next week when it was fully finished.

We then recruited a young and good-looking friend of two of the band members as our singer, called Adam. We also had Andy on guitar, Mark on drums, Dek on keys and yours truly on bass. A keys player was a new one for me, but a superb addition that really added to the band's sound, and he kept his left hand well away from my sonic zone, thankfully. We started rattling off a fair few rehearsals to achieve the legendary 'tightness' all bands strive for. All this actually means is that if someone cocks up mid-song, the band doesn't fall apart during the song and carries on. Oh, and we play in time, and all finish at the same time. Simples.

Tightness achieved, we unleashed ourselves on the West Midlands and had a blast for about two years. Our first gig was in a pub near Solihull and we went down a storm, especially with our version of ELO's Mr Blue Sky. I came to the (incorrect) conclusion that Jeff Lynne from ELO must have grown up nearby, without realising that it's Birmingham City Football Club's fans' anthem. Evidently there were Aston Villa fans (sworn enemies of Birmingham City) at the back of the pub kicking off. Henceforth, we dropped that song in any purely Villa pubs after first checking with the landlord for football club loyalty. One even threatened to set his dog on us if we played it in his pub. Nice.

Many more gigs followed, generally three or four a month, which was great, and also put bread on the table at the time, for some of us hard up folk. I particularly remember one pub called The Pavillions in West Heath, where my position in our standard line up meant I was right next to the Gents toilet door. Every time the door opened and closed, I copped for a lungful of Toilet Duck at best, and something far, far worse, at worst.

It was at this very venue where an extremely rotund chap introduced himself as AC/DC's tour chef. Looking at the size of him, and if it was true, I doubt there was ever much food left for the band, if any. The night went on, and he kept drinking as we played, until the climactic moment where he fell over in very slow motion and gave two of our wives and girlfriends involuntary lager shampoos. It took three of us to get him upright and seated, whilst placating and attempting to dry our rather wet WAGs and complete the set. Angus Young and co must have the patience of a saint. Or this guy was full of crap. Full of something, for sure, and kebabs, pizza and Carlsberg were the hot favourites.

[CHAPTER 10] – GINGER MULE

One night, walking towards a pub gig in a very rough part of Birmingham called Aston with the guitarist, we both heard what definitely sounded like gunshots in a nearby street,

Me: "Fireworks, right?"
Guitarist: "Yup, fireworks."

We ignored the fact it was April, scurried inside and actually had a very good gig. The pub had hosted Laurel and Hardy on the same upstairs stage at an early point in their career, but was set ablaze shortly after we played there in the early 2000s during some civic unrest. Heathens.

After one successful gig in Redditch, the landlord asked us if we'd play at a pub in Bromsgrove he'd just taken over, called The Sugarbrook and we were delighted to get another date in the diary. That was until at least five people at work, who knew the area, repeatedly said "The Sugarbrook? Are you mad? Is it still open? It's a bit rough".

I contacted the landlord who reassured me that it used to be rough, but wasn't any more. He'd recruited the top female door woman from Birmingham's Broad Street (club land) and installed her as landlady, and she'd barred all the troublemakers. I fell for it, and the gig was on.

I was the first to arrive at The Sugarbrook and asked to see the landlady. This female man-mountain descended the stairs, introduced herself and said that tonight was her night off (Saturday night??) and that she was “just a bit pissed”, in the same way that Larry Grayson was 'just a bit gay'. Blindly firkin' paralytically drunk was more like it, and you're our safety ticket for tonight, I thought. Marvellous. She then went for a lie down, and we never saw her again.

The clientele were 'interesting' to say the least, and these were the 'better' ones who hadn't been barred. If you called out their cumulative IQ into a Chinese restaurant, you'd be lucky if they brought you soup. The chief knuckle scraper amongst them approached me when we were set up, looked at the set list and asked if he could sing Alright Now while we played. No harm done, there's an hour to go before we start, and it'll get him onside. Four (vocally murdered) songs later and I'd had enough and told him to stop for 'insurance reasons' as we were going to start soon. I said there's a band on elsewhere in Bromsgrove who love singalongs, and that he could really fill his boots with them.

Him: "Are you telling me to fuck off?"
Me: "Well yes, but politely." (Nothing ventured and in for a penny, eh?)
Him: "C'mon then, we're off."

His kindred Neanderthals left, only to be replaced by several neighbouring tribes who presumably had been fed the same lines I used by other bands in Bromsgrove to move them away from their gigs. Surprisingly, our gig went well, and we escaped intact, falsely promising to contact the pub for future dates, as we left hurriedly.

We were booked for a birthday party in a social club that had an in-house DJ shortly afterwards. When we'd finished setting up, I found the DJ and gave him a set list with the instructions to not play any of these songs, as we're doing them. Sadly, he took this to mean play most of them and wouldn't or couldn't hear our protestations. Come our grand introduction he dimmed the lights and music, and as we, Ginger Mule, stood there poised to entertain, bellowed out "Ladeeez and gentssss, tonight's live band, I give you GINGER MOOSE!!"

It's hard to play an opening song when the whole band is thinking "Where the fuck did Ginger Moose come from?". Our name was at the top of the set list, but he evidently hadn't read that either. Other DJs are available, and avoid that one like the plague, was the lesson learned. Still another great gig, more bookings, we're on a roll. Or rather we were......

At some point in the earlier proceedings we asked the keys player's partner to be our sound engineer and a proper band member on equal pay. He had been very helpful in the early days, mainly due to his access to a very good PA that he could borrow from work, and we did benefit from a front of house sound controller. However, we had unleashed a monster.

> Him: "I'm not doing that gig on the 17th, I need a rest."
> Singer: "I'm sure we can just muddle through ourselves."
> Him: "Muddle?? Muddle??? You think all I do is muddle????"

And thus, Muddlegate was born. After some digestion of humble pie, we assured him that he didn't just 'muddle' and that he was a very important band member (with access to a very good PA). He shortly afterwards declared himself unavailable for all of Christmas and the New Year (yup, prime earning time for bands) as he needed another rest. More gnashing of teeth, but no mention of muddling, that was a definite no no.

Early in the New Year I noticed a Facebook post from our drummer, saying "....and up go the tits, again". I checked my email to find a group mail saying our lead singer was packing it all in and moving to China. That's a bit of a faff, I thought. He eventually left the Midlands and relocated to Croydon, presumably living over a Chinese takeaway, and letting 'bloody autocorrect' take the blame for the misunderstanding.

All the same, he was off. Here we go again, let's get the advert out for a singer. Only there was a problem.

> Muddler: "It won't be the same without Adam."
> Me: "No, but he's a singer, they come and go (a lot, in my experience) so we'll just get another one."
> Muddler: "But we're nothing without Adam. Ginger Mule was all about Adam."
> Me: "Have a collective thanks from all of us for that statement."

The above is a mere précis of what was actually said. It degenerated very quickly into an email war of words, culminating in a particularly poignant/vicious (delete as per your perspective) email from me which pretty much spelt the end of the band. The email features later in this book, in the Bands chapter, Leaving A Band section - you be the judge.

Ginger Mule was dead. The Mule est morte.

[CHAPTER 11] – GOING STRAIGHT

Going Straight was my next project which was pretty much three fifths of Ginger Mule (the keys player sided with his partner, obviously) with a vacancy for a singer. More bloody auditioning. When you are trying to recruit a singer, you do try to filter out the no-hopers, dreamers and mentally unstable as best you can on the initial phone conversation. However, it's not a perfect filtration method.

One candidate arrived with his girlfriend, who was also his singing tutor. Each time he missed a note, she looked at him with severely sharp daggers across the practice room (she'd insisted on sitting in) and we all feared for his safety later that night.

Next up that night was Dave. Very very big Dave. I greeted him at the practice studio reception room where he was sitting. He got up and kept on going up. I'm sure the room darkened as he blocked all light sources, natural and otherwise. He'd better be good, I thought, as I don't want to have to tell someone that big he isn't.

I led him to our practice room for the evening and introduced very very big Dave to the other two band members. Cue my standard opening questions, before the singing bit starts:

> Me: "Have you learnt the four songs I told you to, and are you definitely okay with their respective keys?"
> Dave: "Yes, definitely, and I can't wait to do Don't Stop Me Now" (the Queen classic, like they did some that weren't classics)

Don't Stop Me Now was always the fourth song of four for anyone auditioning, and if they got that far before we stopped them (a mercy killing, in most cases), they were pretty good.

> Me, with question two of about six: "What's the biggest crowd you've sung in front of?"
> Dave, smiling: "Oh about three hundred people......."
> Me, smiling: "Brilliant."
> Dave, still smiling: ".....at my sister's funeral."
> Me, quickly converting a smile to a look of pure sympathy: "Oh great, I mean oh god, oh dear, I'm sorry, errrr....right, shall we just get straight on with the songs?"

Dave, still smiling even more: "Yes, let's go."

I concluded he hadn't liked his sister much, not by the smile, anyway. We rapidly launched into Dakota by The Stereophonics, and I mean rapidly.

If you've ever watched the early rounds of X Factor, you'll be aware that some people really can't sing, only no-one has ever told them. Dave was one such person. Dakota was a real challenge, purely because we were all biting our lips and staring at the floor while trying not to laugh, still very much aware of Dave being very big, and the room being very small, and Dave was between us and the door.

Me: "Err, that was a bit shaky."
Dave: "Yeah, it's nerves man, let's do the next one."

Sex on Fire was even more of a challenge, for him and us but for different reasons, and Daydream Believer was also despatched with a similar lack of anything vocally close to how it should be, and still we stifled the giggles. Just. Personal safety concerns are a great inhibitor.

Me: "You're still quite a bit off key."
Dave: "Yeah, but I'm warmed up now, let's do some Queen."
Me: "Oh god, I mean, oh good."

Don't Stop Me Now was never more inappropriately named, and we lost control. Giggles became tearful hysterics, and any survival instinct was abandoned by all three of us. Thankfully, it ended eventually, or we collapsed in hysterics, unable to carry on - I can't quite remember the specifics, but both were possible and probable. I escorted Dave from the room and to reception and thanked him for his time.

> Dave: "That didn't go too well, did it?"
> Me: "Just get some lessons in mate, and a bit more practice."

There's possibly a singing tutor in Birmingham hating me to this very day for that. However, all I could think of were the mourners at his sister's funeral. It must have been one of those jolly, happy funerals. With him singing, it can't have been anything else.

Despite the other two guys in the band saying "No female singers, they are nothing but trouble", I spoke to Carrie Ann on the phone, was very impressed and booked her in for the final slot on yet another evening of auditioning, without telling the other two guys that she wasn't a he. Cue the dirty looks my way when I led her into the room. And then she sang. Perfectly. And performed each song too. She was probably the most accomplished singer and performer I've ever encountered. She left, we packed down and agreed to meet in the pub next door to discuss that evening's candidates.

Me: "So, no female singers, then?"
The other two: "Err, when can she start?"

I rang Carrie Ann the next day to tell her she was in, and she was pleased. She also said that she was doing a thirty-minute slot on Saturday at a festival in Birmingham if I wanted to see her in action.

Me: "That'd be great, where and when?"
Carrie Ann: "4pm on the stage outside Nightingales nightclub at Pride."
Me: "Ohhhhhh, okay"

My daughter was visiting that Saturday and was well up for it, so off we both went to Birmingham Pride. Once we'd pushed our way through the crowds, and the stalls, and people with chihuahuas wearing dresses in prams, and three men in head to toe latex gimp suits being led on collars and leads by a dominatrix, and all the attractive women with big hands and Adam's apples (I mentally assessed every woman I looked at for the next month at least, for authenticity), we finally found the stage in time for Carrie Ann's performance. She was superb, sang well, really worked the crowd and I couldn't wait for our next rehearsal with her.

And so, Going Straight was formed. The name was a blatant dig at our homosexual former sound engineer, but as our drummer was also gay and said he was alright with it, and especially as I'd recently supported Pride with my custom and therefore wasn't homophobic, Going Straight it was. We launched at a pub in Harborne called The White Horse and a friend in attendance said, "Whatever you do, hang on to her, at all costs". Yup, that good.

We had a really good twelve months of pubs, clubs and parties including one with a front row of cross-legged children. Primal Scream's "Rocks" ("Whores keep a'whoring") was dropped just before it started, appropriately enough. Hell, we even shot a promo video, which is hidden in a dark corner of You Tube somewhere. As a bass player, my view of an audience is often obscured by the back of the singer. With Going Straight, there were plenty worse views to be had than the one I now had to contend with. How we suffer for our art.

Like all good things, it ended. Carrie Ann wanted to turn professional and could do a gig on her own with a small PA and a CD of backing tracks for £200 to £300 or perform for a quarter of that with us. Fair enough, but a shame, nonetheless.

Jools followed Carrie Ann, and was another great singer and yet more gigs followed. By then we'd had a new drummer too, who was okay but a bit lacking in confidence. This culminated in one particularly awkward birthday party gig where he suddenly forgot how to end songs, and stared at me with an increasingly blind look of panic in his eyes as each song progressed towards the end, longing for me to somehow end it. This was the point whereby I realised I subconsciously worked off the drummer's cue to end just about everything. This wasn't going to end well, or indeed, possibly ever.

This peaked with what must have been an eight-minute version of Summer of '69, which felt like the Autumn and Winter of '69 too. Throw in the fact that our then guitarist clearly either hadn't learnt, or had forgotten, many of the guitar parts and the end result was probably my worst gig for many a year. Typically, the birthday girl thought we were great, and paid up. It's amazing just what the average punter doesn't notice. Either that, or she just loved Bryan Adams.

Later that night, Jools and I held an autopsy at Hopwood motorway services on the M42. As good a place as any for an autopsy I suppose, for at least they had hot coffee. No slabs, green gowns or surgical saws, but we made do.

> Me: "That was awful. I'm never going through that again."
> Jools: "Me neither. Shall we just can it?"
> Me: "It's for the greater good."

Hence Going Straight had gone horizontal. Cause of death: an idle guitarist and a drummer with a song end complex. Both were terminal.

[CHAPTER 12] – GUNNRUNNER

In early 2012 I'd answered an ad in a local music shop, and one week later found myself auditioning for Gunnrunner (no typo, just a perpetuated spelling mistake), and got the gig. It was an unusual band in that it started as a four piece, then the singer left (again - it must be me), then the drummer became the singer and we got another drummer. Then the ex-drumming singer left (it is me; it has to be) and we got another singer. Then he left (now I really do have a complex) and the guitarist became singer and guitarist (if he goes, we're totally shafted), and we successfully ran as a three piece for about five years (phew). I remember the guitarist saying how do you feel about me being the singer as well as the guitarist. Apparently, the drummer and I had the same thought (one less mouth to feed, so there'll be a pay rise) and readily agreed.

Gunrunner was really Steve the guitarist's baby, complete with revolving door policy, as demonstrated above. That said, he was a terrific guitarist and a decent singer too and handled both tasks pretty darn well. The drummer was bloody good too, and we made for a very accomplished trio that gigged extensively. Steve was into his motorbikes and had some good connections with various clubs, and we often played to an audience of Sons of Anarchy lookalikes at their rallies and clubhouses. Despite the look they were and are terrific guys, and there was never a whiff of trouble at these gigs. The occasional whiff of an aromatic herb or two, but no trouble. Ever.

Career highlights with Gunnrunner? Here goes, complete with memorable moments.....

> One of those early singers said to a very attractive young lady in the front row at a gig, who'd caught his eye "Well hello, pretty lady, what's your name?"
> "It's Jodie, and that bass player stood behind you is my dad." she replied
> "Ohhhhhhh" said the now sheepish and soon to be ex-singer

The Feathers pub in Lichfield has a great band area, and the landlord loves to work the lights and sound from a control booth out front. Oh, and the smoke machine. Just before we were due to start at our debut gig there, he dimmed the lights and started with a long introduction to us, over the PA. All the while, in the darkness, we could hear a hissing sound and got that familiar smell of stage smoke. Cool we thought, until the lights went up, and away we went. Only, we were up to our bloody knees in smoke. We couldn't see the pedals, nor the set lists on the floor, nor even our feet or any underlying trip hazards like foldback speakers, cables and mains sockets. Hence for the first thirty minutes we stood perfectly still, afraid to move in any direction. As a bass player I'm not supposed to move much, and generally don't – that night I daren't.

(At a later gig there with another band the smoke machine was mounted on the lighting rig over the very drummer's head and blew straight at him. There may have been a request for the landlord to fill the smoke machine with mustard gas, but that's all it was, merely a request)

After we played at an opening night for a new bike club faction, the club President approached me and the drummer to thank us personally. He held out his hand in business style handshake fashion but upon grasping mine, quickly turned his hand upwards into the 'rock/biker' style handshake. I was ready for this and went with it, but he then put his other clenched fist hand on the back of my right hand. I mirrored this too, which seemingly was correct. He then said "Rock and roll forever" and to my eternal shame, the most macho thing I could think of was, "Yes, let's hope so, eh?"

The identical handshake ceremony with the drummer didn't go quite so well and turned into a very bizarre game of 'push me pull you' almost coupled with rock, paper, scissors. The President then moved on for further presidential style duties elsewhere.

Drummer: "That was....different."
Me: "What just happened there? Are we married or something?"

At a late-night open-air bike rally, we were going down really well, and one particular chap was dancing fervently to ZZ Top's Sharp Dressed Man and waving something in time to the music. When we finished the song I looked in his direction and gave him a smile and thumbs up, just as the lights changed and illuminated the thing he'd been waving, which was quite clearly a prosthetic leg and I assumed, his – well, it's not the sort of thing you'd ever lend to someone, is it? My smile and thumbs up were quickly replaced by an "Urgh, fuckkkk!!!" and we rapidly moved on to the next song.

There has to be a special mention here for one elderly biker I noticed wandering around the place, complete with all the biker regalia i.e. boots, jeans, t-shirt, leather jacket, and the obligatory belt with all his keys and chains hanging off it. The special mention is because I noticed that amongst the keys and chains hanging off said belt, was his Tesco Clubcard. Every little helps, indeed.

We headlined at The Robin 2 in Bilston several times, which was very prestigious, thoroughly enjoyable and poorly attended, but hey, it's The Robin 2 and we're playing it. It matters to us amateur rock gods. Following in the esteemed shoes of Carol Decker and T'Pau, or seeing Fish's set list still stuck to the changing room walls does give you a buzz.

At one gig at The Robin I'd manhandled my Ampeg 6x10 cab and amp onto the stage (no mean feat, many complaints from my back, but it's all about 'the sound') and commenced the sound check, only to notice a burning smell and smoke coming from my amp, which promptly died.

Me: "Oh fuck."
Sound engineer: "Do you have a DI pedal?"
Me: "Yes, thankfully, a Sansamp."

The small pedal was placed on top of my tall, heavy and very dead rig, wired up and fed through my fold back speaker. In all honesty it sounded terrific, even though I had the biggest pedal stand in the world, albeit with one tiny little red light at the top, from the Sansamp. "If only we'd known, eh?" said my spine.

At one canal side social club we were told to bring our own PA, but that they had a lighting engineer. I'll bring my lighting rig just in case but leave them in the car. Fewer things to carry in, and all that. When we were setting up, the lighting engineer appeared, plugged in a 9V DC adapter to the mains and the black curtain behind us, and switched it on. This illuminated about twenty tiny dimly lit static fairy lights on the black curtain, and he promptly disappeared, job done. I headed for my car to start bringing all of my lights in. If that guy was paid, I want his job.

The Hinksford Arms near Wolverhampton was a regular gig for us, and the location of an incident that Spinal Tap would be proud of. Just to set the scene, we played along the far wall of the pub which had windows from waist height almost up to the ceiling. Through these windows you had a view of the raised beer garden lawn. Important point - when our drummer sat down, the top of his head was in line with the lawn, albeit on the other side of the window. Okay, scene set.

We'd had another great night there, churning out gems like Wishing Well, Pretty Woman (rock version, of course), Jumping Jack Flash, Gimme All Your Lovin', Whole Lotta Rosie (of course), Rosalie, and Copperhead Road, all to a pretty high standard, and we had almost finished our climactic version of Freebird to much dancing and fervent drunken involvement.

Unknown to us, in the darkness outside, a dog had wandered across the raised lawn through the window and stopped directly in line with our drummer's head. It then arched its back and somehow triggered the motion detect sensors outside for the lights, which then fully illuminated the dog as it proceeded to do a pretty significant 'number two' which, to our audience, looked like it was landing on our drummer's head. The hysterical laughter and pointing followed and cut through Freebird completely, and as Steve and I looked behind us, we joined in. Only the drummer, the target for the 'jobby through the glass', was oblivious but we did explain afterwards - we at least owed him that, and the event shall forever remain in my memories under the label 'Freeturd'.

At one rehearsal Steve proudly carried in his new amp, a 100-watt version of the 50-watt amp he used to use. He endeavoured to get 'his tone' but wasn't totally happy with it. One week later he reappeared and claimed to have cracked it. He told us he'd taken two of the four output values out. “So, you've just converted your 100-watt amp to a 50-watt amp by halving the output power stage, which is what you had originally”, I stated. "No, it's.....different....and better", he said. "Fair enough" was my reply, not entirely convinced.

He then proceeded to A/B the channels and asked me for my preference, having played the same chord twice, once through each channel. "I prefer the second one as it's more bassy and that's my thing, but I guess you prefer the first one as it's slightly more trebley and cutting" I replied.

On to the drummer, same chord played twice, once through each channel, same question, very different answer. "I'm a drummer, I hit things with sticks, I can't answer a complicated question like that" was his answer. Respect due.

Shortly afterwards, and Steve was off on holiday to America, for his annual sabbatical. Apparently, whilst queuing and moving slowly through some US airport customs hall, the lady behind him said “I know you, but I can’t quite place you”. A jetlagged Steve wasn’t too keen to pursue the conversation, and just smiled as he was waived forward to the business end of the customs hall. As he presented himself to the airport officials, he heard the lady behind him shout out “I’ve got it – GUNNRUNNER!!” whilst pointing at him. Of all the places where you would not want to be identified by that label, a US customs hall full of armed police must rank pretty highly. Fortunately, he managed to explain the situation away well before any rubber gloves and lubricant were called for.

By now (2016), I'd also joined a Britpop band (see next chapter) thinking it would be easy to be in two bands, so long as I managed my diary well. It was for a while, then it really wasn't, so I had to choose. I chose Britpop.

[CHAPTER 13] – COMMON PEOPLE

In early 2016 I saw an ad for a Britpop start up band, and thought I'd give it a go. Although Gunnrunner were fairly busy, I did fancy playing something different to the rock classics I'd been doing for the last five years or so. I'd missed most of the '90s music, having been busy with babies and nappies and stuff, and it appealed to me. The band was the brainchild of Bruce, the guitarist, who thought there was a gap in the local market/band scene, and who also wanted to relive part of his youth.

The songs for the audition were Roll With It, Disco 2000 and Common People. So, two root note chuggers and one slightly more complex song. We met at Base Rehearsal Studios in Stourbridge, and I was introduced to Rob on drums and Darryl on vocals, by Bruce. Fifteen minutes in and we'd played all three songs perfectly and I'm sure, silently thought "What do we do now?", for the rest of the two-hour booked session. We played them again, and then just chatted about 'the way forward', an essential part of any band's formation that invariably means learn more songs and try to get lots of gigs.

Rehearsals went well, and we added two of Bruce's friends to the line-up, Dave on rhythm guitar and Clive on keys, as we strived to get a pure Britpop set up and running. (Incidentally, Bruce was really called Dave as well, but we called Dave Bruce to differentiate between Dave and Dave. Clear enough?) When we were almost gig-ready, the singer left (not a-fucking-gain, this is beyond fucking funny now, and a Meldrew stylee "I don't BELIEVE it") for personal reasons. They were explained, and I fully empathised with him, but what is it with me and singers?

However, this time I had a plan. My next-door neighbour was a decent bloke, a good muso, and could sing, and quite fancied the role. One successful audition later and Russ was in, and Common People was (were?) complete. Russ quickly nailed the set, and we unleashed our pure Britpop set on the good people of Droitwich.....to mainly indifference, bar the odd request for 'some AC/DC'.

We tried again at The Olde Black Cross in Bromsgrove, with similar results, and packed our gear away dejectedly at the end of the night. We were just about to start loading out across the patio and through the beer garden when it all kicked off. Just as I reached the window by the exit door, a couple outside were having an argument, and he chose to hit her. Parental love is natural but bottling the man who just hit your mother probably isn't. Still, the son struck. Someone else then bottled the bottling son, and off it kicked. "Best give it five minutes or so lads, it's a bit.....interesting out there", I said.

Police and ambulance appeared later, with the police trying to work out what had gone on, and who to arrest, and the noble paramedics trying to glue people back together. "The landlord will pay you, when he's finished reviewing the CCTV with the police" said the barmaid. It's going to be a very late night, I thought.

Leaving aside the 'Wild West' antics outside, we were still acutely aware that our perfectly honed set list just wasn't working. Indeed, it may even have inspired violence. Perhaps the warring couple had fallen out over the merits of our inclusion of Richard The Third, by Supergrass? Or Hey Dude by Kula Shaker? I guess we'll never know, but the police may have known, if it actually made its way onto a taped statement and was perceived as incitement by the assailant.

Whilst focusing on pure Britpop, we'd failed to realise that obscure songs by the likes of Supergrass were very much 'on message', but off the any 'good songs to play in a pub' list. "Play something we know" had been shouted out several times at the gigs. It generally works better when the band play stuff they know, truth be told. That said, the drawing board was revisited, the parameters slackened somewhat, and we built a set list of 90s hits that were Britpop or Indie, or just popular. Brand dilution for sure, but if the brand ain't selling......'nuff said.

It worked a treat. You can't hate Angels when the entire pub are singing along to it, nor Chelsea Dagger, nor Take Me Out, nor Sit Down, et al. We had about three years of mainly fabulous gigs and some festivals and parties, the highlights (and lowlights) of which were as follows:

In 2016 I made the long-suffering Paula my second wife. I was divorced from my first wife by then, so it was legal and proper. By long-suffering, I mean someone who has had to deal with lots of Friday and Saturday nights home alone, and who has taken delivery of more than her fair share of guitar shaped boxes, frequently unannounced. Then there's the rehearsal nights, and the practicing on your own in your muso room nights, too. There's the irritating retrieval of plectrums from both the washing machine and the tumble drier, and the garage being full of bass speakers, PA speakers, lighting rigs, and an assortment of rugged black bags and cases. There was the testing of a smoke machine in the kitchen. There’s even the return from a cruise holiday to be greeted by a guitar-shaped box on your doorstep as you’re still unpacking, clearly purchased mid-cruise from somewhere on the high seas. Err, not once, but twice. Then there's gigging at your own wedding. Sorry, darling, love you.....but I digress....back to the plot.

We had a lovely ceremony and reception at The Curradine Barns near Droitwich on a gloriously hot day in August, and had a band booked for the evening. Most people were outside enjoying the warm evening, so the band were playing to err, no-one. A well-paid band at that, and worse, we were the ones well-paying them - oh the irony. As arranged, when the band took their break between sets, Common People took to the stage for a five-song cameo, with an exceptionally overdressed (for a gig) bass player. The room suddenly was packed to the rafters with all of our friends and family, and it was my shortest, and best, gig ever. It culminated in us playing 95% of our final song Sit Down, before we managed to trip the sound limiter that the pro band had managed to avoid, and the room descended into silence, then laughter and cheers. A truly magical day.

My wonderful mother, having finally seen me play live with a band for the first time ever, said "Actually, you're not that bad". Fine praise indeed from a wise woman. After 35 years at it, I was finally 'not that bad'. Onwards and upwards, let's push on and strive hard for 'mediocre' next.

The River Rooms in Stourbridge loved us, and my wife and daughter were present to see it. A stage, a back room, a DJ who avoided our set list, a sound engineer who didn't muddle, a lighting engineer who worked off the set list and 300 people loving it, and drinking lots. Heaven, at last! My wife was almost tearful saying "At last you had the audience you deserve". Top woman, Paula. My daughter took some great photos, which quickly made their way to our website - nice work, Jodie, the daughter, and Russ, the singer and web designer.

The Barnt Green Inn in Barnt Green (naturally) was another success. The village is generally populated by the important and wealthy folk who work in Birmingham but don't want to live there. A role reversal for the village, as it was originally built to house the servants of the important and rich folk who worked and lived in Birmingham, but who preferred their serving folk not to live there. Oh, the irony. I too once lived there, but clearly under false pretences. Anyways, it was a particularly sweet moment when Russ sang the Common People line "I want to sleep with common people like you" while pointing at the audience, with an approximate nett value of umpteen millions. Priceless, even.

(At a short-lived start up bands' first and only gig in 2019, our singer/guitarist sang the same line to the massed ranks of his family and friends, at his brother's 60th birthday party. Boy, did that feel awkward!)

Shropfest at Ironbridge in 2018 was another special gig. Unexpectedly, the England football team had actually put a run together and were progressing nicely in the World Cup, and were now through to the quarter finals, against Sweden. We were booked for Shropfest and due on at 4:30pm, whereas the England match kicked off at 3pm on the same day, an incredibly hot day as I recall. There was a massive screen showing the match at the opposite end of the field to the stage. Hence, approximately 3,000 drunken revellers were watching the match, which was going rather well for England, and 'David Bowie' (not the real one, he died in 2016, do keep up) performed a cracking set of hits to err, no-one. As did we, for the first 15 minutes, and then it happened.

The whistle went, England had won 2-0, beer, cheers and arms went up in the air, and then the entire 3,000 headed to watch us play and join in dancing and singing. Another career highlight to make a grown man moist, and then some. As we left via the treacherous stage staircase, avoided the circus guys on stilts (baffled me too), crunched our way across all the empty mini gas cylinders and passed the men fishing near the parking area who were clearly too stoned to detect a bite, I thought to myself "This is the life - eat your heart out, Bowie, we nailed it proper". And, we'd all be home in time for Casualty on BBC1. The gift that keeps on giving, eh?

On the other hand, the Sunshine Festival near Worcester, also that year, could have gone better. We were stopped by security at the artist's entrance (ooh missus) and asked for the band name. Tempted though I was to say, "Atomic Kitten - it's been a very hard year", I didn't, stated our Common People-ness, and we were let in.

The organisers had insisted on a purely Britpop set, despite our evidential based protestations that it generally doesn't work with a typical crowd, and thus we found ourselves playing to very few people, and even they were struggling with the lesser hits of Supergrass and The Seahorses. We retained these few followers, us being their preference over Atomic Kitten on the main stage (flattered and not, please rearrange), but even they moved on when Bad Manners took over from Kerry Katona and company. At least 'Bowie' would have known how we felt, anyways.

Later that year, and more prestigiously, we were booked for a private party at the Bishop's Palace in Worcester, no less. Okay, the party was for our rhythm guitarist's girlfriend, and therefore we were a shoe-in for the band, but let's just gloss over that bit. Just prior to the gig Clive, our keys player, had witnessed the demise of his Apple laptop. This was used to store both essential tones for certain songs that would be utilised by his keyboards, and err, other stuff that we never quite fathomed out. Said sickly laptop was replaced by Clive's wife's Windows laptop, which he used as a backup for the vital tones and other odd noises.

Mid-gig and all was going well. We then started a song by Supergrass called The Sun Hits The Sky which had a keyboard solo in the middle which Clive both emulated and played particularly well. Hence, no concerns on our part as the keys solo approached. The concerns started about two seconds into the solo, which to all present, sounded like it was being played on the world's most poorly Stylophone (something else Rolf Harris should have been imprisoned for).

Apparently as Clive's solo approached and he went to call the appropriate tone from his wife's laptop, the laptop chose just then to display the message "Windows has updated and is now rebooting - please wait". The fact that "I told her to turn off automatic updates" carried little weight at that precise moment in time for Clive as he scrabbled around within his keyboards for a tone, any bloody tone, for the solo due in about 5 seconds. I guess 'Sickly Stylophone' was as far as he got when the time ran out, so Sickly Stylophone solo it was, whilst stared at by five other band members all mouthing 'WTF??' Still, the moment passed, and it was a great gig all told. Whether Clive's wife received her lesson on 'The Inherent Dangers Of Windows Automatic Updates' as soon as he got home, or the following day, was never revealed but I'm pretty sure it happened.

Once in a while us covers bands get to grace the same stage (not quite at the same time, though, but at least the same day) as some of music's greatest ever living talents, and sometimes discover that they are lovely, humble, really pleasant folk, and the three day festival at the Bay Horse Inn in central Hereford was not to be one of those 'whiles'. Common People were booked for a 90-minute slot at 2pm, opening on the last day of a three-day festival, to be later headlined by none other than The Wurzels. Be still my beating heart, eh?

We arrived at noon and went to discuss setting up with our contact there, the sound engineer, who was as far removed from 'happy bunny' status as is possible. He'd built a PA sound system that had worked perfectly for two days. However, earlier that very morning, he'd been visited by The Wurzels' sound engineering team (who knew?) who insisted his PA was taken down and replaced by The Wurzels' PA, backline and drum kit, to ensure The Wurzels' quality control, presumably. He then had to rebuild his PA in front of theirs, for the rest of us low-life bands to use until The Wurzels' headline slot later that day.

We sympathised with him and enquired if we could at least use The Wurzels' drumkit and or bass speakers and or guitar speakers - we're not that fussy. The reply was "I don't know, they've all fucked off to get some breakfast and now aren't answering any phone calls at all".

With time running out we thought it best to load our own gear in, and setup in front of The Wurzels' gear. This second version of everything in front of the first version of everything meant that we had about maybe two feet of performance area left to stand on, play, perform and jig about. Despite the space, we had a pretty good time, whilst not moving much, and the crowd really enjoyed our standard fare of Roll With It, Song 2, Wonderwall, Dakota, Dizzy, Parklife, Friday I'm In Love, and Ruby, amongst others.

Whilst performing we were further developing our loathing for the offending sound team, with each slight collision, edge of stage wobble and accidental coming together of instruments. Afterwards, we actually met them. Three, as I recall. Young, pleasant, well spoken, very upright and each one sporting a sinister, dark rucksack on his back. If ever there was a stereotypical West Country happy clappy Christian Fundamentalist suicide squad, this was it. I knew how this could end......"We're ever so sorry about this, but we'll all get to see God together, and much sooner than planned. It'll be really rather jolly"....then 'Booom'!!!!!! ......so I gave them a wide berth.

As we started to load out we were asked to move our cars by a security man, from the alleyway next to the pub, as The Wurzels' luxury camper van containing them themselves was approaching and would be parking there. He went on to say "I'm security, not a fucking car park attendant " Fair point. They gained many friends that day, not. We duly obliged, 'they' arrived, parked up in the alleyway and never left their van, even as we repeatedly struggled to squeeze past it carrying the usual multitude of heavy black boxes, bags and cases, and endeavoured to keep the skin on our hands rather than leave traces of it on the alleyway's rather abrasive and non-hand friendly walls.

I'm sure their fans enjoyed their performance later, but really, two hits in 40 years, one original (Scottish?) member still in the band......you ain't The Beatles, chaps. A week later my (oblivious to this) sister-in-law went to another festival, had a great time and posted a video on Facebook of the "brilliant" Wurzels singing Ruby ("Ruby, Ruby, Ruby, Ruby, Ruby, ooh arr, ooh arr, ooh arr"). Et tu, Brutus/Jane?

Then there was the black-tie gig at 'The Belfry', the prestigious hotel and golf club that once held The Open golf tournament. We were booked for the West Midlands Small Business Society's Christmas bash. We arrived, setup and soundchecked, then had about three hours to kill. Although we were then told we could have full use of the facilities, none of us had brought our trunks, and a round of golf in the dark had no appeal, so we generally lolled about the bar area. The other guys had brought their own sandwiches, but I thought I'd just get a bite to eat when I got there. I think I blew my entire night's pay on one sandwich and a latte - I did say prestigious.

At one point we found the table-plan for the evening. I'm guessing the person who created it hadn't quite graduated from their Events Management degree course, as we spotted that next to the West Midlands Asian Business Network table was the table occupied by UKIP. This could make for a fun evening, we thought. It didn't, and it wasn't. At the peak we had about six people dancing but put it down to the friction in the room caused by the table planner.

Later that month we were back in Bromsgrove at a nightclub called ‘57 Monkeys’, for no obvious reason. We had to do two sets of 45 minutes starting at 9pm, then clear off promptly as the club then became a disco. All was well with the arrival and load in, and the manager told us to set up in front of the foldaway wall facing the seating area, which we did.

However, at 8:58pm, the manager then decided to fold the foldaway wall away, and asked us to rotate our line up about 180 degrees to the right, for reasons known only to him. A ball-ache for sure, but we complied, just. When I say we, I didn’t include our drummer, as there was no way he could rotate his entire drumkit in two minutes. Come 9pm and off we go, with five band members now playing and looking at the audience, whereas our drummer was still pointing in the wrong direction and remained that way for the entire gig.

You don't realise how much you rely on the cursory glance over your shoulder at the drummer when a song starts or ends, until the time comes when every glance just gives you a great view of the back of his head. That was a very strange night.

One pub in a rough area of North Birmingham was linked to the boxing gym next door, and thus the gym was our pre-performance green room. There's nothing like the smell of sweat and Ralgex to inspire a performance. No recreational drugs for us, unless we cared to raid the industrial size bottle of Deep Heat next to the toilets. That's the blood-spattered toilets, to be totally accurate. I think I'll wait until I'm home, was the collective thought.

Performance under way, all going well, and everybody was happy, which was good, given the reputation of the neighbourhood and the general look of our clientele that night. Especially happy was the chap at the front, and seemingly local hero, who extracted his todger from its natural home, gave it half a dozen rubs and then persistently attempted to shake the hands of Dave on rhythm guitar, Russ on vocals, and lastly, me. I wasn't perturbed at being last, nor were the omitted band members (Freudian?) perturbed at being omitted. I've also never been prone to violence, but this was the closest I've ever been to dishing out a 'size 10 boot' into someone's chops from the elevated stage, as were the others. Fortunately, he returned his todger to its place of rest, and any potential riot that would have undoubtedly ensued was averted. This certainly wasn't in the advert for 'bassist required'.

Another even less salubrious pub gig later (three doormen) and we had one punter doing press ups to Disco 2000. Jarvis Cocker would have been so proud that his tribute to unrequited love inspired such physical exercise. Later that night Mr Fitness then entered the stage area while we were having a break between sets, and tried to talk into the muted microphones and was eyeing up the equipment. I approached him and requested that he move away, for 'insurance reasons' or whatever gibberish I thought appropriate at the time.

> Mr Fitness: "I weren't going to nick anything."
> Me, letting the 'weren't / wasn't' error go uncorrected: "I'm sure you weren't, but there's a lot of fragile gear there that we need to keep the music going, so it's best if you step away from it, please. Why not do some more press ups or star jumps, or something?"
> Mr Fitness: "Okay."
> Me: "Phew."
> Mr Fitness: "Do you want to fight me?"
> Me : "Oh fuck."

Doormen are so called because they are invariably on the wrong side of the door when the trouble starts.

Tonight was no exception, with all three of them chatting to some women outside.

Me: "Not really, as we both know who'd win. Why don't you grab another beer before we start playing again, and you can do some more of your cool PE dancing?"

Potential kicking avoided, and sarcasm clearly wasted, but it's interesting how you can play an entire second set while still keeping an eye on one individual throughout, just in case.

My penultimate gig with Common People was at The Nailers Arms beer festival at Bournheath, near Bromsgrove. It was a bitterly cold and wet evening, and we were to play in the smokers' bus shelter-type shed in the beer garden, facing out to the audience. The cold was challenging enough but for the second set the rain really came down, running off the roof of the shelter and pouring like a waterfall just in front of our faces. Think Duran Duran, and The Reflex video, but on a very low budget, shot in the Arctic Circle and with a band trying to decide whether electrocution or hypothermia would see them off first.

As per, Russ, our singer, announced in early 2019 of his intention to quit but he said he'd honour the gigs in the book. Other singers please note - that's how you do it. At a band meeting shortly afterwards Bruce, the guitarist, said he was off too, for family reasons, but that he'd also honour any booked gigs. So far, so good. New guitarist and female singer brought in, rehearsals well underway, all going well, then the new singer quit. Aaaaah!

> Drummer: "I reckon it's her husband's doing. Shall we have a meeting?"
> Me: "With or without her husband?"
> Drummer: "No, I meant just the rest of us."
> Me: "Ohhhh, okay."

Then I quit. It really must have been my turn by now. I too said I'd honour the gigs in the book. Professional, see?

The background to my quitting was quite unusual. My wonderful wife and I had sold the house, but couldn't find one that we liked. Neither of us was too enamoured with our day jobs, and we had speculated about working together and running a B&B and had even done the odd Google search. Oh, and we'd often visited the village of Dunster in Somerset, and loved it.

Cue 3am one Wednesday morning in February 2019 when we both couldn't sleep, and I ran the Google search again, and found Millstream Cottage B&B in Dunster was up for sale. We viewed it that Saturday morning, loved it, and that was that. Offer made and accepted. I quit my day job (well, it makes a change from being made redundant) by giving my notice in before noon on April Fool's Day.

> Management: "Are you serious? This is a wind up, right? A B&B? April Fool, eh?"
> Me: "Yes, I'm bloody serious! I really mean it!!"

Suitably convinced, I worked my notice period and on April the 24th 2019 we moved from the West Midlands to Dunster, and took over Millstream Cottage B&B. Another chapter in life was over, and another one about to begin. (That's your cue to turn to the next chapter; literally.)

[CHAPTER 14] – THE ROGUES

The Dunster music scene isn't massive. It really consists of a duo called 'Minnie Hates The Hoover' (singer/guitarist and singing drummer), and that's it, bar the odd church choral do, and an annual mini-festival at The Luttrell Arms. There's a few pubs in nearby Minehead that have bands on, and then there's Butlins for the "I used to be quite famous, let's have another go and call it nostalgic" brigade. It wasn't looking good.

Having established this, I placed an ad on the Join My Band website for both the Somerset and Devon sections. My former ads in the West Midlands section generally got about two hundred views in the first week or so. Both ads down here managed the grand total of seven views in the first week. This is going to take a while.

I honoured the final Common People gigs in the Midlands, including two that were on successive nights; that was a killer, or rather the commuting to and from them was. Still, commitments fulfilled honourably, let's find a band. Hey, it's what I do.

There was a brief flirtation with a start up in Weston-Super-Mare that read well in the ad, and sounded good on the phone, but fell apart at the first rehearsal for me. The Indie band quickly became alt/indie versions of rock songs that aren't in that genre (what??) without warning. This, coupled with the band rules emailed to me the day before, and I was out.

The rules included such gems as:

- We are people first, musicians second (fine, whatever that actually means)
- Our family comes first (no shit, Sherlock)
- Avoid divorce (more sound advice)
- Cheesecake at rehearsals (seriously???)
- No use of drugs or loose women whilst performing (rather tricky I'd say, but let's not be too hasty, eh?)
- Respect each other (nope, I'm gone)

There was more, much more, but that, and the first rehearsal, was more than enough for me. I was out of there quicker than a turkey at a Christmas party. Another bullet dodged.

Then came the phone call from Martin, lead singer of The Rogues, a Barnstaple-based covers band, with a bassist vacancy. We chatted and clicked on the phone on a Sunday, met for a rehearsal on the Thursday, then gigged on the Saturday night. Skin of my teeth and all that, but it went well / I got away with it (delete as applicable). So, more rehearsals and a lot of practicing, and we're now gigging regularly, have done pubs, parties, some festivals and a wedding, and have quite a few gigs and festivals already booked for this year. One such festival to come is ‘The Sands Of Music’ in Westward Ho! in Devon, where as per last year I’m told, we appear on the advertising as The Rouges. Red faces all-round, I suspect.

The final icing on the cake was an invite to join Minnie Hates The Hoover for a six song guest spot at a gig at ‘The Stags Head’ in Dunster, my local, which morphed into 18 songs at the next gig.......which has just been cancelled due to Covid.

Currently bands, gigs and life in general are on hold due to the Coronavirus lockdown. We have a B&B with no guests and no income, but hey, “Always Look On The Bright Side Of Life”, as the song goes. It'll pass, touch wood, and we'll all come out of the other side hopefully better people. And the whole rinse and repeat band stuff will start yet again.

Edit: During this Coronavirus lockdown, we now have a thing called 'Clap For Our Carers'. A very noble and well-deserved activity, with a most unfortunate title. The idea is that for about five minutes at 8pm each Thursday, we all stand in our doorways, or on our driveways, or even hang out of windows, and generally clap, cheer and bang dustbin lids and the like, to show our appreciation for the good people of the NHS during these difficult times.

Last week a friend and his wife took part for the first time. They stopped watching their TV just before 8pm, moved outside to their driveway, and clapped, cheered and banged on the lid of their bin. When they stopped, they realised no-one else had joined in and came to the conclusion that all their neighbours were miserable buggers of the first degree. They returned to watch their TV, realised that they had been watching it on catch up, and were one hour later than the rest of the UK with their clap-fest. And yes, he's a drummer.

Music and musicians - the gift that keeps on giving.

PART TWO

Welcome to part 2, and I'm glad you made it. What follows is an number of chapters, based on specific themed topics from the world of music and bands, and peppered with more anecdotes and humour; for example 'guitarists' and my experiences with them. You may learn something, or even agree with my entirely biased perspective (hey, it's my bloody book after all) and find it kinda reassuring that we all encounter the same fun and games in the world of cover bands, but if all that I can get from you are smiles, giggles and maybe substantial belly laughs (that's substantial laughs, not substantial bellies) based on my experiences, then I'll still regard it as a job well done.

Reflective point coming up. Even after all these years, and bands, and gigs, and songs, I still have this inner feeling that I'm not a 'proper' bassist, and that one day someone will point at me and shout this out at a gig, and I shall be rumbled. In the meantime, I'll keep faking it and console myself that when I approach our front door minus a key and have to ring the bell, the Nest doorbell announces that "There's a friggin' rock god at the door". Mind you, it was me who keyed it in and linked it to my face, via the facial recognition option. Little things, and all that.

[CHAPTER 15] – BASSCHAT

I can't write this book without both mentioning and heaping praise on Basschat. You can find it at www.basschat.co.uk and it's an online community for us bass players. There's advice, discussions, events, help and perhaps most importantly for gear magpies such as I, a marketplace for all things bass. It's well moderated, and generally a nice place to spend time online.

Oh yes, the marketplace. I thought I was fickle with the way I keep rotating basses and amps, but I now know I suffer from a thing called Gear Acquisition Syndrome, or GAS. Fortunately, almost everyone else on Basschat also suffers from GAS, so I am amongst friends. Everyone on the forum is protective of their feedback and reputation, and after twelve years of wheeling and dealing on there, I've never had a bad experience nor met a fellow Basschatter I didn't like. That is a slight problem in that when we meet to do a sale or swap which should take about ten minutes, we almost invariably spend several hours just chatting about all things bass.

I dread to think of how many deals have been struck in car parks and motorway service stations over the years, and I suspect that everyone's collective gear on Basschat has almost moved round the entire forum at least once, so I should be getting some of my early stuff back soon. We must be good guys, because I recently did a swap at Oxford train station during a security incident. That's two blokes with basses in gun shaped bags on their shoulders, meeting in a station that's crawling with armed police. The trade went ahead, and all was well, but all movements were very very slow and deliberate, just in case.

Most deals are struck at halfway points such as motorway service stations. Just try to avoid the following phone conversation:

Me: "I'm here, by the main doors"
Seller: "Me too, but I can't see you. Wave your arms about"
Me: "I can't see you either, and I am waving"
Seller: "Yep, gigbag on shoulder and nope, still can't see you"
Me: "Oh shit, hang on. I'm at the northbound services. Are you....?"
Seller: "....at the southbound services"

There wasn't a footbridge either.

[CHAPTER 16] – BANDS

In my unprofessional opinion, a band is two or more musicians at the same place and same time, playing the same tune (except for jazz, when they all play different tunes at the same time). However, this doesn't happen by chance and much as we all want and like to be in bands, there's a few basic stages to conquer first to ensure a successful, productive and peaceful future. Here are the key ones, plus other stages that may follow:

Assembling - someone, or maybe more than one, has to decide to put a band together. At this critical point they need to be sure what they want to achieve. It may just be a singer / songwriter who wants to perform their original songs once a month but needs a backing band to give their tunes a bit more clout for a live audience. It may be a few friends who want to put a reggae band together, and gig extensively. Whatever the objective, be clear about it. Then, when you start advertising for members, auditioning them, agreeing a setlist and finally getting out there and gigging, everyone is on the same page, and an awful lot of grief will be avoided. There'll still be grief, guaranteed, but lessen it if you can.

Be specific about music genre, covers or originals or both, band line up, number of rehearsals and gigs a month, where you want to gig, the look, potential recordings and videos, media presence, any potential band purchases and how any earnings will be divided up, and or re-invested. With all of this in place, you can then advertise for the musicians your band will need and commence auditioning prospective candidates. There's a whole chapter on that particular ball-ache process coming up.

Naming and social media presence - assuming auditioning went well (hah!), and you have your line-up, you really need to get a name together sharpish, and the accompanying website, and Facebook and Instagram pages. Oh, and get used to the following question, like it matters: "You're in a band – what are you called?"

The list of names of bands I've been in, and can still recall, runs something like this: Maximum Volume Band, Cemetery Gates, England In Flames, Mid-Life Crisis, No Worries, The Usual Suspects, Rock Monster, Ginger Mule, Going Straight, Gunnrunner, Common

People, Clive's Birds, Go Indie!, IndieGo, The Rogues, and Minnie Hates The Hoover. Some had very descriptive properties and some were just pants, and hasn't everyone of a certain age been in bands called Mid-Life Crisis and The Usual Suspects? An easy solution is to link together two disparate words such as Ginger and Mule, or Arctic and Monkeys - one worked much better than the other.

Trying to slip a word about your musical genre into your band name may work, but rock, pop and indie have been inserted into so many band names they probably now need lubricant. A tribute band name can also be a challenge, but dyslexia can be your best friend, as in Ion Maiden or NoWaySis. My all-time favourite is a Meat Loaf tribute performer who goes out as Pete Loaf.

Your band name really needs to be unique - if you impact on a successful band with the same name it can get messy, and you'll be the ones who have to change. Also, the name will already be in use on social media, thus causing you further problems when you come to promote yourselves. When your social media pages are up and running, lean on as many friends and family members as possible to get the Like and Share counts up quickly - savvy pub landlords are now looking at your alleged popularity before they risk booking you for the first time.

It also helps if you can establish a look, however you choose to implement it. Loud shirts, smart jackets, camouflage trousers (can never find mine), just anything that you're all prepared to wear but more importantly, will differentiate you from the rest of the people in the pub or club. Look like a band - they're paying you for this!

Band purchases – I've almost lost track of the amount of gear….okay, PA systems, that I've contributed to as a joint band purchase, only for them to become either very contentious issues, or just plain old stolen, when a band splits up. It's also messy when just one person leaves and wants their 'share'. If they leave nicely, you'll feel obliged to see them alright. If they are fired, or just quit leaving the band in a mess, you won't. As Judge Rinder always says, "Where's the contract? Where's the agreement?" It comes to something when I'm quoting him, but in this instance he's right. So, before you all chip in and go shopping, you may want to crib or adapt the following agreement that I finally drew up before my last joint band purchase:

BAND AGREEMENT, TERMS AND CONDITIONS

Description

This is an agreement between the members of the band xxxxxxx to establish and protect the band's assets and monies, and the respective members' interests in these assets and monies, and to put in place pre-agreed strategies for members leaving the band.

Members

As of 28th of January 2018, the band xxxxxxx consists of:

Dave, of address, postcode
Dee, of address, postcode
Dozy, of address, postcode
Beaky, of address, postcode
Mick, of address, postcode
Titch, of address, postcode

Assets

As of 28th of January 2018, the band's assets consist of the following:

1 x Allen & Heath Mixer/Amplifier PA12-CP #serial number here, with an approximate value of £375

2 x 20m Speakon to Speakon cables, approximate value of £120

2 x speaker stands, approx. value £50

2 x EV ELX115 PA speakers, with covers, approx. total value £350

Subsequent assets to added here, with date and value:

- *Future asset 1*
- *Future asset 2*
- *Future asset 3*

Monies

As of 28th of January 2018, the band's held earnings consist of:

About £125, held by Dozy

Subsequent held i.e. banked, not distributed, earnings to be added here, with date and amount:

- *Earnings 1*
- *Earnings 2*
- *Earnings 3*

Leaving the band – voluntarily

It is deemed that voluntarily leaving the band may be caused by one of the following reasons, although this list is not exclusive:

Change of interests, moving away from the area, health issues, discontent, disharmony,

In the event of any of the above situations happening, the member who wishes to leave must submit their resignation in writing and honour any pre-booked gigs wherever possible and to the best of their abilities. Failure to do so invokes a total submission of the resigning member's claims on any band assets and monies.

In the event of any outstanding HP payments incurred for the purpose of purchasing band equipment that has been agreed by all band members, and that have been initiated or are mid-term, then the departing member must honour their outstanding personal element of that payment, either monthly until the HP loan is fully paid up, or in full, unless the majority of the remaining band members agree that this is not necessary.

Upon receiving a termination letter and that member's subsequent departure from the band, a majority of the remaining members will agree to reimburse the departing member for their share of the assets and any monies held, at a time that is agreeable to them, and no longer than twelve months from receipt of the resignation letter.

<u>Leaving the band – involuntarily</u>

If the majority of the band members decide that one member is not performing to the standard that is required for reasons that are within that person's control, they can insist that the person leaves the band immediately, and they will be issued with a termination letter signed by the majority of the remaining band members.

In the event of any outstanding HP payments incurred for the purpose of purchasing band equipment that has been agreed by all band members, and that have been initiated or are mid-term, then the departing member must honour their outstanding personal element of that payment, either monthly until the HP loan is fully paid up, or in full, unless the majority of the remaining band members agree that this is not necessary.

Upon receiving a termination letter and that member's subsequent departure from the band, a majority of the remaining members will agree to reimburse the departing member for their share of the assets and any monies held, at a time that is agreeable to them, and no longer than twelve months from issue of the resignation letter.

Joining the band

Anyone joining the band can be asked to buy their way in and to donate an equal share of any band assets that they will subsequently have use of. They will not have claim to any monies already earned and held; a new agreement will be drawn up and signed pertaining to an equal share of any monies earned for all members from the day of the new agreement onwards.

Closing the band down

If a majority of the band members are in agreement and all sign a statement to that effect, the band is in effect ended. Any held monies will be divided evenly between the band members, and any assets will be sold as close to market value as is possible, and the money again divided evenly between the members. A single member or members can purchase any or all said assets if desired, but at a value that the remaining members all agree to and share equally between themselves. A minority of the members can continue with the band using the band name and social media presence, and can purchase any or all said assets if desired, but at a value that the original members all agree to, and share equally between themselves, if the majority of those who don't wish to continue are in agreement.

We, the current members of the band known as xxxxxxx understand the terms of band membership laid out in this agreement and agree to comply with them in their entirety.

Dave – agreed, signed and dated:
Dee – agreed, signed and dated:
Dozy – agreed, signed and dated:
Beaky – agreed, signed and dated:
Mick – agreed, signed and dated:
Titch – agreed, signed and dated:

The signatures above were witnessed by:

Name:
Signature:
Address:
Date:

It ain't perfect, but if and when the sticky stuff hits the fan, it's a whole lot better than nothing, and should be good enough for a Small Claims Court exhibit.

Managing - managing a band is like herding cats, only not as precise. By managing I don't necessarily mean getting a manager in to err, manage stuff. A band needs a leader, and the founder member generally takes that role, or passes it on to someone more capable when the first opportunity arises. Democracy is a wonderful concept, but seldom works with humans, and even more rarely with musicians. And when it does, it still doesn't. Example:

Four democratic musicians form a band and sit down to select a song each for their first four song rehearsal. Very democratic so far. All four nominated songs have to be included, 'cos that's democracy. However, one song is an absolute bitch to play and get right, one has a massive brass section throughout (how are you going to pull that off?) and the other two songs will die on their arse in front of an audience because they are either obscure, not that catchy or just crap.

Still, democratically it was a success - good point well made?

Back to the band leader it is, then. Someone needs to take charge and keep things moving along, point out what areas still need work, but also point out when things are going well and progressing. This can and often does breed resentment, so needs to be delivered in an empathetic and positive way, rather than using a 'Stalin on a bad day' method of delivery. Example:

> Band leader: "That bass line isn't quite right. Do you need a bit more time with it, or do you want to come round mine one night and see if we can crack it?"
> Bassist: "Yeah, I'm struggling with it a bit. How about Tuesday night and I'll do some digging on YouTube beforehand?"

This is a good way to progress.

> Band leader: "That bass line is pants, and sounds like a three-year-old child is playing it"
> Bassist: "Pick a window short-arse, you're about to go through it."

This is not a good way to progress. Although fictional (bassists need far more provocation to react to anything at all), it should get the point across succinctly.

Finally, if someone is still not responding to a nice style of correction with encouragement and sensitivity, sack the twat. It saves time. Harsh but fair, and they had their chance.

Turning professional - although this is the dream for most of us weekend warriors, the reality is rare, and often harsh. A friend and ex-professional muso said the practicalities of being pro were gigging in city A, and hoping you sell enough t-shirts to get some food and enough fuel to get to city B for tomorrow night's gig. Oh, and sleeping in the freezing cold van yet again.

Good luck if you are doing it, and fingers crossed that it works out for you. If it doesn't, the world of Mustang Sally, Valerie, Sex On Fire and Sweet Home Alabama will always extend a warm welcome.

Leaving - sometimes life throws things at you that mean you have to leave a band, and sometimes you've just had enough. Either way, try and leave in a helpful manner by giving plenty of notice and offering to cover whatever gigs you can, until they have a replacement for you. If the situation has become untenable, at least give it some thought before you actually pull the trigger, unlike this guy who detailed his departure on a forum:

> Unhappy bassist: "I'm sick and tired of you lot - you never actually learn the songs properly enough to play them well, you're just a disorganised bunch of rabble that is going nowhere. I'm gone, screw the lot of you."

He rapidly bagged his bass guitar and amp and stormed out of the practice room without a second glance. Five minutes later, he reappeared.

> Unhappy (and now humiliated) bassist: "Err, could someone give me a hand out with my Ampeg 8x10 speaker cab, please?"

Note to all - always consider the hissy fit quit properties of any potential purchase.......or wait until you've loaded out, and then quit in the car park.

Alternatively, if the band are adamant that they want you out, go. No point in staying where you're not wanted, and another band will come along shortly.

Finally, when a five piece band falters because the singer, then another muso and his sound engineer partner also decide that they are off, you may decide that you want to let off steam with an email to the entire band, as I did with this:

"Guys, I've spent much of the last six months feeling awkward and biting my tongue for the alleged greater

good of the band. However, I tolerated things (no matter how bloody annoying they were) and got on with it, believing that we had common goals. I put my personal irritations aside and tried to be professional, reasonable and conciliatory. The fact that you can't do this saddens me but doesn't surprise me.

Here's a few home truths and suggestions you may wish to cut out and keep, should any of you decide to dip your toes into band land ever again (and please, think long and hard about it, as your next band might not be so tolerant, reasonable and fundamentally accommodating of your foibles, whims, failings and fancies):

- *You don't become a £1,500 a night band by putting your prices up and waiting. You become what's known in the trade as a band with no work. It might have been rather more helpful if you had chased down some of your friend's high earning band's venues and tried to get us in there*
- *You're in a band. It will do gigs. Accept it. Don't moan. It's what bands do. You should not be surprised by this. Think raison d'etre*
- *Small gigs lead to bigger gigs. It's happening now. You should have stuck with it. The small ones are a necessary part of this process*
- *It doesn't take forever to get a band banner organised. We could have commissioned the*

original team that did the Bayeux Tapestry for a quicker result

- *A band with some lights is visually better than a band with no lights*
- *A band in a pub ideally needs some lights. It doesn't need a mains-powered version of the aurora borealis complete with resident lighting engineer, on a total budget akin to the GDP of Switzerland*
- *Being in a band is a good, fun thing. Moaning about stress and pressure just indicates that you don't belong in that world. Stick to moaning about your day job, and leave band vacancies for people who will enjoy it*
- *A sound engineer in a small band doing pub gigs is a nice-to-have nonsense. It should be the role of the singer to buy and manage the PA. The rest of the band has bought and manage their own respective equipment*
- *A sound engineer dictating what gigs we do, and when, and for how much, is a complete nonsense and the ultimate manifestation of the tail wagging the dog*
- *A sound engineer spends approx. 45 minutes setting up then effectively has the rest of the night off bar one or two tweaks. He is not on display, nor does he have to be word / note perfect for the best part of two hours. He incurs no rehearsal costs. He should not be taking an equal share of the night's takings*

- *If a venue books you, it is not necessary to 'do a recce' to see where the mains sockets and doors are. It's a reasonable assumption that there will be mains sockets and doors somewhere*
- *It's not appreciated to refer to the cost of said 'recces' as an incurred expense, when they aren't required (see point above)*
- *A local band did a gig on a Friday. There were pictures on their Facebook page the very next day. We did a gig in September and paid (yup, bloody paid) Allan to take pictures. So far we've had one picture. It was a nice picture though*
- *If you offer to work your notice in a band, keep to your offer especially if other people are being fair and reasonable towards you*
- *Just because other people in a band aren't bitching and moaning all the time, it doesn't mean that they are happy with what's going on, nor does it give you the right to walk all over them*
- *The expression "Ooh, no John, no band" is technically incorrect (as is about to be proved) and is also extremely belittling, derogatory and downright insulting to all people not called John in the band*
- *The expression "John's leaving, we'll get another singer" is technically correct (as is also about to be proved) and is therefore not flippant but factual. For the record my last band, over twenty years, had one guitarist, one bass player, two*

drummers and at least eight singers. They leave. It's what they do

- *The expression "He's so much more than just a singer" could possibly be perceived by some as nothing more than sycophantic drool, as it appears to be merely because he does some (very nice) artwork sometimes, and sometimes some of his friends and/or family come to see us. We all do and did other stuff, and we all had friends turn up*
- *I think it's a reasonable presumption to make, that band stuff conveyed to Joe would reach Allan, as they lived together. The channel clearly worked very well in the opposite direction*
- *When you walk out on a band, you walk away from your share of the collateral – that's just how it is*
- *And when someone is going against tradition and is making a reasonable offer despite your walkout, don't throw it back in their face*

With regards to specific individuals:

John – you're a good singer, but only an okay front man. I fully anticipated this course of events to a certain degree when you auditioned, which was why I wasn't really in favour of you joining. I expected your life to move on a bit and it did, and for the band thing to be surplus to requirements, and it was. Enjoy your travelling and good luck in the future. Perhaps now after reading all these words you can appreciate that others can put their personal irritations to one side and get on with things for the sake of the band or the greater good; it's a shame you couldn't manage to do that

Joe – I believe that you said you were thankful for the band, as it gave you the confidence to get your current job, which is a wonderful thing. However, it was becoming more apparent that the band had served its purpose for you, and that you too wanted to move on. It would have been nice if you'd offered to make your departure less sudden, or acknowledge that I had left things with you until you were fit enough to discuss

Allan – none of this will come as a surprise to you I'm sure, but whereas you see yourself as someone who speaks up, stands up for themselves and won't be dictated to, the expression 'over inflated sense of your own worth' seems to sit well with me. You come from a background where unions were quite embedded, and workers were allowed to feel like they mattered and had a voice and could say whatever they felt because it mattered to them. However, that world is going, as I think you're seeing and have seen, and in the business world you wouldn't last five minutes. You lack tact and diplomacy, and are too pre-occupied with getting your own way and what matters to you, often at the expense of the thoughts, wishes and feelings of others, for you ever to sit in a team of differing free thinking individuals

We did have a band of people who were primarily conciliatory and considerate, and who discussed things. You ploughed in with 'shan't', 'won't', and 'non-negotiable' whenever things didn't suit you, irrespective of anyone else's perspective. You also seemed to take on the task of fan club chief and personal ego masseur to John without realising that the band was never called 'John and some lesser people who don't matter much'. Your extracurricular stuff was useful yet more often than not you then undermined it with a stance or hissy fit over something that had to be right for you. Muddlegate was really fuelled by you creating doubt and uncertainty with John's ability to manage a PA and any PA problems, and sing, yet most bands of our size and level do muddle through perfectly well without a sound engineer. Certainly not one who then attempts to elevate himself to a position of dictatorial authority only surpassed by Hitler, Stalin and Mao, or so it seemed

Paul – what to say? Top guy, great drummer, and someone I'd love to work with in the future

I've probably said far too much and will now be a wanted man in parts of the West Midlands. However, this feels like a very English thing to me in that I've suppressed my thoughts and feelings for so long, that when I finally voice them, there's much to say.

And having sat back and listened for a long time to a whole load of self-centred whinging, moaning and griping from an inner circle of self-important individuals fundamentally more concerned with the creation of a mutual admiration society, it would appear I have much to get off my chest. But that's it gone now. I am cleansed, and boy does it feel good"

Please note that sending an email like this will undoubtedly kill any chance of a reunion ever occurring, but I felt it had to be done.

[CHAPTER 17] – AUDITIONS

There are two elements to this, auditioning others, and when you yourself have to audition.

Auditioning others - nowadays you can advertise for free for band members with a Facebook post, or on sites like Join My Band or Gumtree. Alternatively, you can spend a few quid on paid alternatives like Bandmix. Homemade ads in practice studios and music shops can also reap results. However, you source your required band members, always make first contact with a phone call. This way you can easily reject the first-round no-hopers, and if it's a singer you're after there will be plenty. Bloody X-Factor has instilled delusions of adequacy into many a socially inept, tone-deaf, talentless muppet, and they will contact you, guaranteed. A phone call is preferable to being in a confined space (such as a rehearsal room with only one door) with them, when their failings become apparent. A few useful questions to aid the filtering process:

- How long have you been singing / drumming / playing in bands?
- Which bands have you been in before, and why did you leave?
- Do / did they have a website and Facebook page, and are you on it?
- Are there any videos of you in these bands on YouTube?
- What's the biggest audience you've ever played to?
- What gear do you own?
- Can you drive, and do you own a car?

You'd be surprised how many can't scrape through these round one questions. If they are a band virgin and it's their first foray into our world they too might not fare well with the above, and it's entirely up to you on whether you want to persevere with them. Occasionally it works well, often it doesn't, and either way it will take longer to achieve something with them, rather than someone with experience; it's your call.

Round two (gulp) is you invite them to an audition, probably in a rehearsal room at a practice studio, but ideally somewhere neutral. You don't want them knowing where you live, just in case. Nominate three or four songs, ideally varied in style and key, from your set, and email them the MP3 files of the song versions you're doing. You don't want someone waiting for the five-minute intro on the dance mix to end and come in, when you're doing the three-minute radio mix. Also, advise them that the song keys will be as per the MP3s sent, if possible, and especially for singers. Just for singers again, tell them that it's not a memory test, and feel free to bring printed lyrics if they need them. Tell them all the address, and what they'll need to bring (for non-singers) such as snare, cymbals, guitar and lead, etc. Finally, give each singer a 30-minute slot on audition night, and an hour for other musos. Some won't show and vanish off the face of the earth, anyways. Then, on said day and at said time, the nightmare begins......

Most non-singing musos turn up on time and generally do their thing without any issues, whereas with singers it's very often 'different'. If I had a pound for every time the following scenarios played out, I'd have quite a lot of pounds:

> Me: "Did you print out the lyrics?"
> Singer: "No."
> Me: "Okay, so you know them?"
> Singer: "No, but I'll get them up on my phone."
> Me: "You'll be the first person ever to get a phone signal in this room, but feel free."
> Singer, five agonising minutes later: "I can't get a signal."
> Me: "No shit."

And:

Singer: "You're playing the song in the wrong key."
Me: "We're playing it in the same key as the MP3 I sent you - did you use that to practice to?"
Singer: "No, I used a version I had on my iPhone."
Me: "Which, it would appear, is in a different key, yes?"
Singer: "Err, yes."

It's worth remembering that these are people who are trying to impress us - it's very easy to forget. Then there are those who just can't sing, and those who claim to be nervous and singing badly because there's three of us listening to them, while we play. If three's a problem, it doesn't bode well for when we are gigging, although I have done gigs where three was the number of people in the audience, but I digress.

Auditioning - now it's your turn**.** Assuming some git like me has spoken to you on the phone, and it went well and you've been invited to audition, make sure you have obtained the following:

- Date and time of location
- Postcode and address of location
- Songs, versions and their keys - MP3 if possible
- What you need to bring

Don't attempt to learn twenty songs for an audition, as I did once. Five minutes in, and I realised I really didn't like the other guys in the band, and they weren't all that good. That was a very long two hours I'll never get back. Three or four songs is more than enough for both parties to form an opinion. Oh, and don't make inappropriate jokes, like my drug dealer joke with the three musos in the police (oops).

[CHAPTER 18] – REHEARSALS

Rehearsals are an essential part of band life, particularly in the early days. You can ease off a bit when you're up and running to say, fortnightly, but the more you play together, the tighter you get and the better you sound. You can also develop the subconscious ability to play your way out of a mistake mid-song, whether or not it's your error. This is the kind of confidence and being at ease with the setlist that can only come from repetition. Mistakes can and do still happen, but you come out of them better.

It's worth having a structure to a rehearsal, even if it's "Next week we'll play the entire first set several times". You can also throw in new material (that should have been learnt at home first) and any 'corrections' from your last gig. Here are a few examples of lessons learned:

Me: "Right chaps, this week's homework is The Monkees and Believer, in the recorded key."

One week later at the next rehearsal, and after no issues were reported back to me and I was feeling good about it:

Me: "Okay Monkees and Believer, give us a four count on the sticks and let's give it a go."

What followed was an unholy musical mess and car crash of the first order, rightly aborted in well under a minute. A round robin question session revealed that no-one had any issues practising at home at all. Only, half the band were perfect with Daydream Believer, and the other half were perfect with I'm A Believer. The two do not sit well together, especially at the exact same time. Hands up, my fault totally. My bad, even, if I were younger. We eventually put both songs in the set list and they worked well, especially when we all played the same song. Thereafter, I sent an MP3 to each band member of the song or songs dished out for homework.

More recently, I requested that we had a go at Don't Look Back In Anger at a rehearsal as it had sounded a bit naff at the last gig. The singer said "No need, cracked it. Our rhythm guitarist has admitted that he was playing Champagne Supernova for the first half of Don't Look Back In Anger". Glad we cleared that one up, then.

Rehearsals are also places for making ‘interesting’ discoveries, such as this one. A few years ago, at a rehearsal, I called out the next song to be done as Hush, by Kula Shaker.

> Keys player: “We’ve just done that one.”
> Me: “No, we’ve just played Hey Dude by Kula Shaker.”
> Keys player: “Well I’ve been playing Hush, even if you lot haven’t.”

Thus, we discovered that the keyboard parts for those songs are interchangeable.....or we didn’t notice how ‘out’ they were. One of those statements must be true.

A big plus nowadays for rehearsals is we now have the ability to record them easily. I bought a Zoom H4n hand recorder, but mobile phones can also suffice. Place them with care in the room, so that you get a balanced mix, and record a copy of anything new, or that needs work. Afterwards you can then email the recording to the rest of the band, and fine tune your bit at home, or identify where it's going wrong.

[CHAPTER 19] – THEORY, AND PRACTICING ALONE

Theory is a non-sexy subject and, to a degree nowadays, theory knowledge can be deemed optional. In my early days of classical guitar, I learned how to understand staves, and time signatures, and keys, and various note lengths, and where the notes were on the guitar neck. Now, I've forgotten most of that, and I get away quite well without it.

If you want to go down that particular route, there's plenty of books, tutors and online tuition available that will explain just why this note follows that note in any given progression. As I recall, if a note doesn't follow the rules, it's called an accidental. The thing is, it's still there, flying in the face of alleged musical theory regarding scales and keys, and permitted to be there by virtue of its accidental label. So much for the theory rules, then. Summarising, in theory, theory is theoretically essential. In practice, it doesn't need to be. Theoretically, that is.

Alternatively, if you just want to play songs, there's this thing called tablature which is pretty much playing by numbers. Each string is represented by a straight line, and the number on the line tells you where to fret it on the neck. There's a mass of tablature, or tab, out there on the Internet and most of it is free to access.

One word of warning though, some of it was compiled by students of the Les Dawson School Of Piano Playing and thus at the worst possible time in a song, and for maximum impact, the tab will indicate the worst possible note to play at that point, as per Mr Dawson's piano playing. He was very clever and did it for comedic effect with an audience. Some of the free tab on the Internet has also been compiled by clever people, but for their personal comedic enjoyment, while they wait for the next series of Doctor Who to air. Hence, if it sounds wrong, it probably is - use your ears, rather than blindly trusting the tab.

Even if you are making good progress with your tablature 'playing by numbers' approach, it's still worth knowing the notes on the neck. It really helps with tuning, and avoids awkward moments like this:

> Guitarist: "That bit isn't right - I'm playing C minor augmented 7th, what are you playing?"
> Me: "Err, I'm playing 3, on the second fattest string."

There's also a lot of freely available chords and lyrics on the Internet too. Generally speaking, there's enough free stuff out there to get you spot on, or at least close, to the song you're trying to learn.

One device I'm happy to endorse as probably the most useful bit of muso kit I've ever bought, is the Tascam MP-BT1. Load your MP3s into it, plug in your guitar and headphones, and play along. Change the key, change the tempo, slow down the busy bits, loop just the busy bits until you've got it sorted, add effects......you get the idea. There are similar devices out there, and various apps too, and all will aid home practice no end.

[CHAPTER 20] – SINGERS

Oh boy, where do I start? There's been a few good 'uns along the way, and an almost endless supply of muppets. Consider this:

Phil is a bass player. He has several bass guitars, and a bass amp, and a bass speaker cabinet. He's spent about £3,000 on his gear.

Bill is a guitarist. He has several guitars, and a guitar amp, and a guitar speaker cabinet. He's also spent about £3,000 on his gear.

Jill is a drummer. She has a drumkit made up of 5 drums and 5 cymbals. Jill has also spent about £3,000 on her gear.

Will is a singer. Will has a bottle of water, a microphone and some lyrics that are all kept in a high-quality carrier bag. Will's total outlay is £71, plus 10p if he had to cough up for the carrier bag. Will has auditioned for the band made up of Phil, Bill and Jill. If Will gets the job, he will want everyone to chip in for the band PA, as he doesn't see why it should just be him paying for it, claiming "We'll all be using it". No, we won't; at least, not as much as you'll certainly need to.

Will gets the job with the band, and the band all pay 25% each of the cost of the new PA. Will can't keep the PA at his place as he has no room, nor can he transport it as he only has a small car. Will hides around the corner when rehearsals are on, and watches as the band carry the heavy PA in and set it up, plus their own gear. Will then saunters in with his high-quality carrier bag, and rehearsals commence. At the end of the rehearsal Will can't help with the load out as he has something on that night and has to shoot. Will thinks he's the best thing about the band, anyways.

Will is just about every bloody singer I've come across, bar a few notable exceptions. The trouble is, no singer = no band and no gigs. They are a necessary evil. If you can get a good one, hang on to them and treasure them.

Mind you a good singer is no good if they stand rooted to the spot and introduce each song like a historian. "This next song was released in 1982 and was on the album called The Gift. It's Town Called Malice, by The Jam" isn't going to make your audience particularly moist now, is it? What you want, what you really really want (sorry), is a good singer who is also a good frontman or woman. Someone who chats and interacts with the audience, who gets them singing, dancing, laughing and cheering. I've worked with a few of these types, and it's always entertaining. Here's some examples:

All The Small Things by Blink 182 has a quiet-ish middle eight three chord interlude before we all come back in for a raucous end on the pre-chorus. Our current singer frequently goes into the crowd with a tambourine during this bit, and gees them up perfectly, then dashes back on stage for the ending. It's a joy to watch, only a few gigs ago we lost sight of him completely. We repeated the middle eight constantly and played around with the tempo until, after about five minutes, he reappeared, and we finished the song. At half time, we enquired as to where the f.....he'd gone. "I needed a leak, and afterwards had a quick look at you guys. You seemed happy enough, so I went outside for a quick vape as well" was the reply. Priceless.

Next gig, a wedding, and the same song. This time we kept a close eye, and he didn't stray too far. At the correct moment, he hot footed it back to the stage....only his new shoes slipped on the shiny floor, his legs went from under him and he fell, seemingly in very slow motion, flat on his back. Like true pros, we thought we'd better stay on the middle eight just a few more times until he regained composure and joined us for the ending. He then went on to round up about eight bridal party members for the Mustang Sally "Ride, Sally Ride" bit. Shameless.

Years ago, at a biker gig, our flirtatious singer was getting a bit too flirty with some of the females in the audience, enjoying the freedom his extra-long microphone lead afforded him. Our guitarist got hold of the lead, and slowly reeled the singer back in to the stage area, for his own wellbeing.

[CHAPTER 21] – GUITARISTS

Rhythm guitarists - let's start with the easy one first. Dedicated rhythm-only guitarists are calm, pleasant, charming and accommodating folk, who I've always enjoyed the company of, both onstage and off. Our current rhythm guitarist is considerably bigger than me, but that in no way affects my opinion of them.

Lead guitarists - this is going to take a whole lot more words, and applies to most, but not all, lead guitarists, so here goes:

- Why do they need to be so bloody loud?
- What is this unwritten rule that if it's louder it's better?
- Why do they always soundcheck without engaging any pedals and get the levels set, then proceed to stamp on every darn pedal in front

of them the minute their first solo is due, and thus boost their sound by a factor of 1,000?

- Why do they take a Marshall 4x12 cab and 100W valve head to an intimate pub gig?
- Why all this fuss about 'my tone'? Your tone is fucking loud, and anything else is indiscernible

That'll do for starters, but there's more. Much more. Most of the ones I've known have been fastidiously correct about theory but filling your brain with a myriad of scales, chords and modes comes at a price. This 'filling' seems to squeeze out other stuff, like emotional intelligence, compassion, consideration for others, and any care-free attitudes that their personality used to harbour. Why else do we get interrogations like this, at the end of a very successful gig?

Guitarist: "Who missed the C sharp Minor in the chorus of Angels?"
Me: "Who cares? They loved it."
Guitarist: "I care. What are you playing over the 'protection' word?"
Me: "Err, G sharp - I don't do minors. I'm on bass. I do roots."
Guitarist: "That's wrong."
Me: "Same key, and it's the fifth - near enough for me......and they loved it."
Guitarist: "I give up."
Me: "If only you would......"

This level of forensic analysis and microscopic attention to detail can even extend to their backing vocals. We had one who said he'd take the Spanish verse in 'Should I Stay Or Should I Go' by The Clash. He then pointed out that it wasn't just Spanish, but Ecuadorian Spanish. Who knew? Who gives a f....and when I suggested that he could just sing a list of Spanish coastal resorts and airports for all that audience would know or care, I was most royally shot down in flames.

Back to the volume thing. In my first band our guitarist had a Traynor valve amp that we always complained was too loud. His line of defence was that it was only on 3 (out of 10), on the volume dial. I bought that amp from him, and used it for bass, and discovered that there was no difference whatsoever between 0.1 and 10 on that dial. It was a bloody switch, either off on 0, or firkin' loud on any other setting.

Still with the volume thing, a Queen tribute band I was in that thankfully never gigged had a young and talented guitarist who had the Brian May sound perfected, albeit loudly (no shit). However, he couldn't wait for us to start gigging as he wanted to "Get out there and melt some faces with my volume". Why, oh why do they have to do this?

With one band, during an initial practice setup session with our all new in-ear monitoring system, I was accidentally 'given' the guitarist's mix instead of mine. My mix was roughly 20% bass, and 10% for all other key instruments and singers (keys, lead guitar, rhythm guitar, snare, kick drum, vocals, backing vocals 1 and backing vocals 2). His mix was approximately 97% of himself, and a 3% mix of everything else. Draw your own conclusions.

They are also prone to not listening. I played with one who used a Boss ME50 multi-effects pedal that had an intermittent hum, occasionally coupled with odd interference. Despite repeated requests to get it looked at and fixed, he didn't. It all came to a head when, at an open air carnival with a decent crowd, he pressed one of the switches and launched into his solo, only it was accompanied by live football commentary being broadcast by someone, somewhere, nearby, and amplified through the substantial PA to an amused audience. There had never been a guitar solo that climaxed with ".....and Lineker shoots, and scores!!!" until then, so I guess we made history that day, of sorts.

[CHAPTER 22] – KEYS PLAYERS (KEYBOARD-ISTS?)

I've only played with two so far, but both have been very accomplished musicians and nice guys too. One was even introduced to the audience at the band intro bit as 'The Professor'. The only negative thing that springs to mind was the flight case he kept his mighty organ in, which weighed rather more than a small planet and I'm convinced was a loading ramp for Network Rail in a previous life. Be smart, and go missing when he's loading in and out. I was once asked why our keys player had a laptop stacked on top of his multi-keyboard setup, by a particular irritant from another band who stalked us for a while. "He uses it to catch up on 'Eastenders' during the songs with no keys" was my reply.

We put Long Train Running by The Doobie Brothers into the band set with the other keys player, which has a harmonica solo over one verse in the original. Leave it to me for the gig, he said. We assumed he'd be playing some patch on the keys in its place. At the gig, at the appropriate verse, he reached into his pocket, pulled out a harmonica and played the most perfect solo. A real wow moment for all of us in the band.

Like I said, very accomplished musicians, a pleasure to play with, and they can add a whole new dimension to a band's sound.

[CHAPTER 23] – DRUMMERS

Well, where do I begin? The butt of many a muso joke, yet in my experience they've almost always been great guys. Intelligent, pleasant, committed, skilled and noble allies in the rhythm department battle with the rest of the band. Yes, they do play a bit quicker when you're gigging, but then we all do. They are also pretty strong, as per the nature of their trade. Quite why they cart a massive black plastic case on wheels with them to every gig, I know not. The case is full of bits of plumbing and scaffolding, and must have an inner lining of lead, hence the incredible weight, but it must bring them good luck or something.

I never thought that Stuart Copeland (drummer in The Police) was all that special, until on two separate occasions I saw two very good drummers attempt to emulate his drumming on Message In A Bottle. They both ended up bright red and totally knackered, but worked at it and got there in the end. Mucho respect guys, and Mr C.

One or two drummers do seem to carry more cases than a Heathrow baggage handler on overtime. This invariably means masses of drums, and takes them forever to set up. When they've finished, the remaining four-square feet is left for the rest of the band. It's best to try and reason with them. Some of the best, and busiest, drummers I've worked with have got away with minimal kit. Whereas a Roger Taylor Queen-esque drum roll is impressive, it does come at a price for the rest of us, and you really can't drop those rolls into every darn song.

The heartbeat of their kit, and the band, is their kick drum, yet I can seldom, if ever, hear them. The presence of their lucky pillow inside the kick drum (what's that all about?) doesn't seem to help, either. For rehearsals, just grin and bear it. For gigs, if you can, get a microphone on the kick drum, and get it in the PA but especially the foldback monitors. Better still, get it into your in-ear monitors if at all possible. When that has happened for me, I invariably play the bass slightly differently, and better.

I said earlier that they'd almost always been great guys. Almost. My years of defending them to the hilt ended temporarily for me when we had one certain drummer in a band that I shan't name, who managed to personify every drummer joke I'd ever heard, and add a bit more all of his own. You want evidence? Here goes:

At one busy gig that was going well we were about to start Chelsea Dagger. There's a distinctive drum intro, then I join in on bass, and we're away. Only at this gig, nothing happened. We all turned to the drummer, who was staring at his feet for reasons known only to him, and certainly not looking at the set list. The short-tempered guitarist screamed at him "DRUM!!!!!" so drum he did, albeit with a look of responsive terror in his eyes. However, what he was drumming wasn't the intro to Chelsea Dagger, nor in fact anything any of us recognised, but he'd been told to drum, so he was drumming. I was desperately looking for a beat to hang the bass intro on to, but there was nothing there I could catch. More barked instructions from the irate one came. "Chelsea Fucking Dagger - DRUM THAT!!!" and so with the correct instructions (almost) punched into him, he did, and off we went.

A typical conversation:

> Drummer: "Next week's gig at The Red Lion, where do we park?"
> Me: "I suggest we park at the same place that we did last time we played there."
> Drummer: "Oh, we've played there before?"
> Me: "What have I done to deserve this?"

Another conversation, often repeated:

> Me: "Did you all get the email about next week's gig, and the details?"
> Drummer: "Yes, what time are we getting there?"
> Me: "7pm, it's in the email. Did you read it?"
> Drummer: "Yes. What time do we start?"
> Me: "9pm, it's in the email. Did you read it?"
> Drummer: "Yes. What's the postcode?"
> Me: "B9 4AG. It's in the email, FFS. Did you fucking read the fucking email???"
> Drummer: "Yes. What time do we finish?"
> Me: "It's in the fucking email!!!!! When you said you'd fucking read it, which fucking part did you actually fucking read?"
> Drummer: "All of it. Where do we park?"
> Me: "IT'S IN THE EMAIL. Somebody hold me down before I kill him!"

Yet another conversation:

> Me: "Here's your setlist."
> Drummer: "Don't need it, thanks; I've still got the one from the last gig."
> Me: "That was four weeks ago."
> Drummer: "Yes, but I haven't lost this one."
> Me: "Very good, only the running order has changed, and the two new songs are in."
> Drummer: "Oh, I'll take it then."

And again, just before the start of the second set:

Drummer: “Have you got a setlist?”
Me: “I gave you one at the start.”
Drummer: “Yeah, I’ve lost that one.”

One final drummer story, which still generates a guilt trip, albeit a little one. In the past, a fairly volatile drummer was prone to kicking off over the slightest thing, and the patience of the rest of the band was wearing very thin. He was constantly moaning about new songs to learn, or possible poor attendance at the next gig, or whatever he decided needed moaning about. Two weeks before a prestigious gig he quit, following an online tiff with the singer who effectively told him to “grow a pair and stop moaning all the bloody time about everything”. Peace broke out following an olive branch offering from the singer, primarily to ensure the gig still went ahead.

The gig did go ahead, albeit with a slightly strained atmosphere amongst the band, and it was a huge success, probably one of my most enjoyable gigs ever. The next day we all got a group message from the drummer, saying what a great gig it had been, but that he had pains in his right wrist. My very public reply, via the group chat thread? Well, it was there for the taking really, wasn’t it?

> "Just use your left hand. It'll also feel like it's someone else doing it, so it's a real win win situation"

This was met by silence from the drummer on the thread, although the others chipped in with a few LOLs. One day later the drummer announced that he'd been diagnosed with RSI, had sold his entire drumkit, and was packing in music altogether. Oops.

[CHAPTER 24] – BASSISTS

Bassists are the backbone of any a decent band. They are invariably cool AF, good looking, understated, tolerant, honest, intelligent, decent and remarkably nice.......said the bassist (let's not forget just whose book this is!)

[CHAPTER 25] – GIGS

I don't know about you good people, but this is why I picked up a bass in the first place. I wanted to be in a band, but I really wanted to play gigs, and after 40 years of doing so, I still want to do as many as I can. I get a certain amount of self-satisfaction from practising at home on my own (stop it), but there's still nothing like the buzz of hammering out a set full of crowd pleasers to a pub or club packed full of people having a great time.

The praise, the adulation, the applause, the cheers, the unintelligible requests, the bizarre dancing and even the disdain from the few because "Your (Britpop) band didn't play any AC/DC" is just so addictive. It's my personal feel good power trip that keeps me going until the next gig. It differentiates me from the norm, partly defines me as a person, and detracts from the Monday to Friday drudgery of the working week. Most gigs generate at least one story, incident, memory, mistake or funny that you can dine out on for the following week at work, then it's time to rinse and repeat.

It'll be a very sad day when I finally have to step back from gigging and/or playing. Heck, I might even find out what's on the television on a Friday and Saturday night, although I kinda suspect it ain't good. On second thoughts, I'll just go out and watch other bands, and sob gently at the back of the room. For now, here's a few things I've learnt along the way.......

How to get them - If you can, cut your teeth with a support slot with another band. They may even let you use some of their gear, but don't count on it. I know of one really good bedroom guitarist who discovered he shaked uncontrollably when playing in front of an audience, and promptly retired from gigging forever after two very trembly support slots. Probably best to make this discovery with a small audience, and sooner rather than later.

Assuming your band is free from tremblers and support slots aren't available, try approaching a local pub and offering your band's services for free at a gig in aid of a local charity. I've done this several times, and everybody wins. The band get their first gig notch on the headboard, the pub gets free entertainment for their drinkers and generally sells more beer, and the local charity makes money too.

Whenever you put a gig on, make sure you set it up as a Facebook event, and share it to all and sundry, request that they too do the same, and invite everyone and their dog via Messenger. Many pubs are now starting to look at a band's social media activity and popularity and want to see effort on their part to make the gig a success. I often invite friends in Australia and Poland to my gigs, knowing full well that they won't come even when they click to say that they are, and also knowing that the pub won't dig this deep. There's also no harm in putting a few fictional Private Function gigs on your website on dates that you're unavailable for, in the early days. It makes you look established and busier than you are and may sway a landlord to book your band. Oh, and a week before you play there, give them a call and make sure it's still the same landlord in charge, as they change frequently and the bookings diary often goes missing, and that the pub itself is still open and trading. I've fallen foul to both those scenarios quite a few times.

How to make them a success - make sure you're a good fit for the pub, well before you approach them. A rock pub full of bikers probably won't enjoy a mod band's set. Disco pubs hate rock bands, trust me I know that from experience, and we were lucky to escape intact. See what bands also play at the pub before you try and get a gig there, and go and watch them there, and learn what works and what doesn't. Don't take too much alcohol onboard before and during the gig, but afterwards is fine. If one of the band makes a mistake, don't all turn and stare at them, tempting though it is. It identifies the culprit, adds pressure and advertises the error to the audience who generally don't notice such things.

Be on top of your setlist. By this I mean as one song is about to finish, look at the setlist to see what's next and be prepared for it. Also, have enough copies of the setlist for all, and then a few spare. Good DJs and lighting engineers will ask for a copy and work to them, and your drummer will inevitably lose or eat his setlist at some point in the evening, and thus need another one.

Don't drown the audience with the sound of just one instrument, like maybe a guitar, eh? The audience want to hear a band, not just the lead guitarist with some lesser bit-part players. At soundcheck, set the levels to that of the quietest band member, and keep it balanced. Also, if the guitarist has boost pedals, and they will, make sure these are also set for levels during the soundcheck too. If they have three daisy-chained boost pedals, just keep a pair of wire cutters handy.

Use a wireless, or a long guitar lead, or even a friend you trust, to go out front during the soundcheck and help set the levels. The same friend can also indicate mid-gig if anything needs adjusting on the fly. Singers often tire, and their natural volume drops, so you need someone out front to point it out. It's unlikely you'll hear it where you are. It's unlikely you'll hear much at all where you are. All those years of experimentation and expense in search of 'my tone', and yet at most gigs I'm resigned to the fact that if I can just hear myself I'll be happy, and kiss goodbye any subtle nuances of 'my tone'.

Then you're off. Play well, smile, have a laugh with the other band members (even if you can't hear what they're saying), and look like you're enjoying yourself. This is what it's all about, after all. If you've got a wireless or a long lead, get out there and mingle while you're playing. You're not there to be assessed on your note perfect rendition of Franz Ferdinand's Take Me Out, and you won't get busted by the pub police if you miss a change, you're there to entertain, and also to make the audience thirsty and drink more - it's that simple.

Come the half time break, get out there and mingle some more - that's all of you. Ask them if they're enjoying themselves, is the sound level and mix okay, can we get you dancing later, what songs are you looking forward to, anything at all, but just interact with your audience.

The second set is the one that really matters, and the last thirty minutes even more so. Get this bit right and all that went before is pretty much forgotten and / or forgiven. This is the time for your ultimate big hitters, get the punters up and dancing, and just keep 'em coming (the songs, not the punters, just so you're sure, wouldn't want to get that wrong).

Towards the end of a gig, it's nice if the singer introduces the band one by one, and you all do a mini four bar solo. I used to run through the distinctive riffs for Another One Bites The Dust, or Under Pressure, or Peaches for my turn. When done, hit them with the encore, and stop. Leave 'em wanting more, as they say.

After the gig - when you've finished, get out there and get talking to the audience again, rather than just pack away and promptly vanish. "What songs would you like us to do next time" is a pretty good line - just smile and nod when "Whole Lotta Rosie" is the reply and move on. Again, engage and interact. That's it, you've gigged. Now on to the next one.

It became a tradition in one of my bands to hit the local McDonalds on the way home after a gig. You're sweaty, knackered, thirsty and hungry, but also on a high and too buzzy to sleep, so the Golden Arches it was. Once, sitting in my car with our singer, eating our fast food delicacies at 2AM in the Longbridge McDonalds car park, we had the following conversation:

> Me: "Did I really just see a man dressed as a carrot get out of that car in front?"
> Singer: "Yup."

Me: “Followed by a man in a semi-deflated sumo wrestler costume?”
Singer: “Yup.”
Me: “Cool. Glad it’s not just me, then.”

Here's some random gig stories, mishaps and observations.....

After a very successful recent gig the singer approached the bar manager for our payment, and was told that our bar tab was just short of £300. "Err, what bar tab? We're all driving and have had one pint each" he replied. Seemingly some guys had opened up a band bar tab that was nothing to do with the band, and drunk themselves silly, hopefully at our expense. Thank god for CCTV. The bill found its way to the rightful owners who coughed up and were banned, several bar staff members were reminded that the band were the guys playing all evening and therefore unable to queue up and drink copious amounts while they were playing, and we were off the hook. Bloody good idea though, just wish I'd thought of it years ago.

There's one observation that has always amused me whenever a venue has door staff. These (normally but not always) man mountains are the size of a small planet and pay good money to go to gyms and pick heavy things up and put them down again repeatedly. Not once have they ever offered to pick up any of my heavy things as I go back and forth to the car, loading in and loading out. I wouldn't even charge, unlike their gyms. I live in hope.

A pro friend in a named band (that won't be named but they've toured with Metallica) isn't immune to the odd gig 'oops' moment either, and has detailed two of his high-profile ones:

Incident 1: He miscalculated how far he'd wandered across the stage, versus the length of his guitar lead. There was a pop, then bass silence, in front of 70,000 people at a festival in Toronto.

Incident 2: He wandered out onto the far wing of the stage the next night at the same festival, but paid full respect to the guitar lead length. However, he suddenly found he could no longer hear his bass rig on this part of the stage, just as his solo was approaching. The resultant 'soloing while sprinting back to his territory' was much enjoyed by the rest of the band, and the crowd.

A relative of mine is a teacher at a public school in London, and teaches the offspring of the rich and famous. At the end of the scholastic year, the teachers put on a show for the pupils and their parents. His words "It's nerve-wracking enough playing Crazy Little

Thing Called Love badly on guitar at the show, but I had Brian bloody May in the front row watching me as well!"

I once played at a venue that had just had Steven Segal and his blues band on for the two nights before us, and the staff were still talking about him, and his, err, ways. They'd told him that he could leave the band's gear all set up overnight after the first show, ready for the second show. However, they stressed that the gear needed to be covered by his insurance as the venue's insurance didn't cover it. Steven Segal said, in all seriousness and adopting his mandatory steely-eyed Hollywood hardman glare: "Hey, if anyone touches our gear, people will die". Well really, Mr. Segal. Knowing the locality of the venue, I'd have £5 on the locals any day of the week. Aikido? Type of dog, innit?

Best not to mention the gig I turned up early for, and hastily carried my gear in and got fully set up under the watchful eye of the barman, who then said, just as I started a soundcheck on my own, "You're not on 'til tomorrow night, mate". Thanks – sooner might have been better, pal.

Then there was the gig where we headlined, but the support band were still not showing any signs of starting over 30 minutes after they were due to go on. I enquired when they were going on, and got the rock and roll answer, as follows: "Someone smacked our drummer in the face, and we're just waiting for his nose to stop bleeding and his blurred vision to go, then we'll be on". True professionals.

The things singers have said during our gigs.....feel free to borrow them:

"Good news - the landlord has just lifted the ban on dancing, so let's have you all up on the dancefloor."

To a particularly passive audience - "We're much better with a live audience."

"We've had a few requests, but we don't know a song called 'Go home, yer crap' so we'll have to give that one a miss."

After one shocker of a mistake - "We always do that just to prove we really are playing live - no backing tapes in this band."

As we're about to play Disco 2000 - "Is there anyone here called Deborah? This one's for you." There never was, ever.

As we're about to play Look Back In Anger - "Is there anyone here called Sally? This one's for you" There may have been, but as we used to play Love Is The Law by The Seahorses complete with the line "Strap-on Sally chased us down the alley" earlier in the set, anyone called Sally had probably already taken the decision not to make herself known.

The things singers have said during our gigs, but really shouldn't have........don't ever use them:

"Nice dancing love, and you don't sweat much for a fat lass."

"This next song is Messing With The Kid, by Rory Gallagher, and I'd like to dedicate it to Jimmy Saville" - It gets worse - "I don't know why there was all that fuss about him, he fixed it for me to milk a cow blindfold, when I was seven" - I did warn you. I still cringe now about that one.

[CHAPTER 26] – SONGS AND SET LISTS

The songs you choose to do will define you as a band, be they originals, covers or a mixture. If you're in a tribute band your songs are already defined for you, as is your setlist too, most likely. I can only really comment on covers nowadays (original stuff was a looooooooooong time ago) but the following words may be helpful to some:

- Stick to songs that you can all play, and play well. My current setlist is devoid of any Jaco Pastorius numbers as a) I'm not good enough to play them and b) there's not too many punters in The Black Horse who'd actually recognise the songs and dance to them, fortunately.

- Avoid putting your own favourite songs in the set - once you've pulled it apart, micro-analysed it, rehearsed it endlessly and gigged it a few times, you'll end up hating it as much as I now hate Town Called

Malice by The Jam, with its fiddly bloody riff and tricky middle eight that the drummer cocks up the timing on every bloody time, and that the audience love to bits so in it bloody stays in the bloody set.

- Avoid songs with dominant string or brass sections unless you have a string or brass section, or a keyboard player who can cover those sounds. Alternatively, a backing track may help but that's something I've never tried, nor want to. A guitar-based band churning out Boogie Wonderland by Earth, Wind and Fire with an invisible brass section just looks odd to me, and you start to question just how much is being played live, and how much isn't.

- Try and group your set list into bunches of three or four songs that flow well together, and practice minimising the gaps between those three or four songs. Better still, get them to flow from one to another if you can. There's nothing more tiresome to watch than a song ending, then the singer / guitarist takes a drink, dries his hands, tunes his guitar, turns the pages over in his book of lyrics, adjusts his pedals, has another drink, then launches into the next song.....if anyone is still there. I still cringe now when I think back to that band, those gigs, and those gaps.

- When you've finished each three or four song bunch, that's when your singer can do their amazing wit and repartee bit. Banter after every song also becomes tiresome and kills any momentum you had going previously. If you've got them up, try and keep them up. Just let it flow, as any decent urologist would advise.

- As the legendary (!) McFly sang "It's all about you". Only they were wrong, it isn't, it's all about the audience. If you have to play a song you hate, so long as the audience like it, just grin and bear it. After about ten years off, I'm now playing Mustang bloody Sally again at every gig, and it's always one of the most popular songs of the night, unfortunately. Same with the Rolling Stones and (This Could Be) The Last Time; I always always hoped it was.

- Most covers bands are playing very similar sets, so try and make your versions your own. Vary the tempo, introduce breaks, try call and response vocal sections, middle eight clapalongs, try anything that makes your versions a bit different, and a bit better than the others. A friend claims he once walked past four pubs on a Saturday night, and the bands in each of them were all playing Dakota as he passed by. Ah but, when we do it (and we do), our version is better.

- The first song of each set is generally a throwaway assembly call to the audience, so don't waste any big hitters in these slots.

- Don't be too wary of simple songs just because they are simple. Sit Down, 500 miles and Zombie are all three or four chord songs, yet they get a massive reaction every time we play them.

- Sometimes the entire first set is poorly attended as people now seem to get tanked up at home on cheap alcohol as is necessary while watching Simon Cowell's latest prime time TV offering, then come out to play at 10pm. Don't take it personally, it's happening to bands in High Streets everywhere. Start later if you can, or just treat the first set as a paid practice session.

- Try and get your set list to build to a crushing climactic crescendo (more alliteration, impressed yet?) with a succession of singalong, dancey, very big hitters at the end, and save two or three gems for an encore. This is what they'll remember you by, and you should get an invite back.

- Try and vary your setlist between repeat visits to the same venue

- You can drop an original song in, if you have some. However, in my experience, it is generally a great way to clear the dance floor and kill a gig. I'm not allowing for the fact our originals at the time may have been a bit rubbish - try your own, and see how it goes.

Okay, that's the end of the advisory points, now how about the songs? The following list was cribbed from a Basschat thread (thanks, and credit to Stewblack) about the most crowd pleasing set list ever. There'll be some people out there who'll be a bit sniffy about the following list, as it's not too challenging for them, or too mainstream. My take on this is that if you can play at least half of these songs well, you'll be a shoe-in for most covers bands, and get to do lots of gigs, and help a lot of people have a good time and get paid. Not much pay, but we are the few who generally go into a pub, have a great time and leave with more money than we started with. This is both rare, and to be treasured.

One final pre-list point to make. Remember, rock and pop musicians play songs with three or four chords to hundreds of people, whereas jazz musicians play songs with hundreds of chords to three or four people. I know what my preference is, so sniff away at this little lot, all you competent folk out there:

- Sex On Fire
- Sweet Home Alabama
- Song 2
- Wonderwall
- Mustang Sally
- Dakota
- Sweet Child O' Mine
- Living On A Prayer
- Knocking On Heaven's Door
- Whole Lotta Rosie
- Born To Be Wild

- Play That Funky Music
- Let's Dance
- Smells Like Teen Spirit
- Chelsea Dagger
- Proud Mary
- Summer of 69
- I'm a Believer
- Sweet Caroline
- Johnny B Goode
- All Right Now
- Mr. Brightside
- The Gambler
- Don't Stop Me Now
- Valerie
- Brown Eyed Girl
- I'm A Believer
- Teenage Dirtbag
- BIllie Jean
- Walk This Way
- All Or Nothing
- The Joker
- I Want To Break Free
- Time Warp
- Teenage Kicks
- Footloose
- Basket Case
- Uptown Funk
- Three Little Birds
- Hey Jude
- Country Roads

- Zombie
- Sit Down
- This Charming Man
- Yellow
- With Or Without You
- Creep
- Hot Stuff
- Get Lucky
- Superstition
- Hard To Handle
- Brown Sugar
- Whisky In The Jar
- Town Called Malice
- Let Me Entertain You
- Crocodile Rock
- Brass In Pocket
- Higher And Higher
- Don't Look Back In Anger
- Parklife

The list isn't complete, as he missed out bloody Angels.

[CHAPTER 27] – PUNTERS

A most unusual breed. You could be dying on your arse for 95% of a gig, playing Classic Rock, Southern Rock and Texas Rock Blues covers (I never knew the difference, and I was in the band), yet so long as you finished with Born To Be Wild, Sweet Home Alabama and Whole Lotta Rosie, they'd think you were great, and ask when and where you were playing next.

The more they drink, the better the band gets, and they don't discriminate at the end of a night. We've played Angels very badly, and also perfectly. Either way, it always goes down better than an Eastenders actress in a car park. There's no justice.

Then there's the conversations with the audience..........

Often in Bromsgrove (why I know not), there were often chats with very drunk punters during the gigs along the lines of:

> Punter: "Qrqrrr jjfjfjf shhhhhhfffff vbvbvbvb?"
> Me: "We're playing it later, stick around, you'll love our version."

Another gem, also from a Bromsgrove Common People gig:

> Singer: "There's only two songs left so if you're not already up and dancing, now's the time to join in."
> Punter: "Will you play Common People"
> Singer: "As we're called Common People, and as there's only two songs left, it's highly likely to be one of them."

Bromsgrove again:

> Punter: "What stuff do you play?"
> Me: "Britpop, Indie and other gems from the 90s. Think Blur, Pulp, Oasis, Stereophonics, and even Robbie Williams."
> Punter: "No AC/DC then?"
> Me: "Err, surprisingly not. An oversight on our part, clearly. We'll review the set list tomorrow night at a crisis band meeting."

In Wolverhampton there were the following conversations, post great gig:

> Punter 1: "Are you with the band?"
> Me: "Yes" (Thinks: adulation / autograph, maybe / perhaps just mild appreciation)
> Punter 1: "Excellent. Where can we empty the ashtrays around here?"

Surprisingly, that wasn't on my list of possibles and nor something I could help with. It must be a Wolverhampton thing, because, five minutes later:

> Punter 2: "Are you with the band?"
> Me: "Yes" (Thinks: maybe this time.....a modicum of praise)
> Punter 2: "Cool. Do you have a USB charger for my vape?"

Again, I was unable to help. FFS sprung to mind. So, readers, when you arrive at a pub for a gig, familiarise yourself with ashtray emptying locations and carry a spare USB vape charger, and avoid the mistakes I clearly made on that day.

In Lye, as I left a Halloween gig dressed as the Voodoo Doctor of Death, complete with top hat and full scary make up, and a guitar on my back and a microphone stand under my arm:

> Punter: "Are you with the band?"

Me: "No, this is my regular Saturday night look."

In fairness, praise did indeed follow, and I almost felt guilty for my sarcasm. Almost.

A friend's band used to reckon they could tell which song was about to be requested just by the look of the punter as they approached the stage. "Watch out, here comes Sweet Home Alabama" and they were generally correct. Personally, that’s a way in which I’d never want to be identified.

[CHAPTER 28] – GROUPIES AND ROADIES

Groupies - couldn't possibly comment. Not to protect the sanctity of my perfect marriage, nor for moralistic reasons, nor even for any legal reasons such as defamation of a now established good character and known bastion of the local church and community. Nope, an emphatic and firm 'no comment' it is. This is entirely on the basis of no experiences whatsoever, sadly. Still, early days, and it ain't over until the fat lady sings, and maybe lowers her selection criteria somewhat.

Roadies - see above, but please omit the fat lady selection criteria bit.

[CHAPTER 29] – BASS GUITARS

This is the chapter I hope my wife never reads. Another hope of mine is that when I do pop my clogs, I hope she doesn't sell my basses for what I told her they cost. One bit of advice that I should have followed is only ever buy black guitars, because one looks pretty much the same as another one, to a disinterested spouse, hence you can chop and change to your heart's content. The lifelong quest for the holy grail of tone is what drives this chopping and changing. I've lost track of how many times I've declared my latest acquisition as 'the one' to my good lady, only to sell it six months later because it wasn't, but the next one coming in will be. My selection criteria with bass guitars is this:

- It has to look good
- It can't be too heavy
- It has to be nice to play sitting down
- It has to be nice to play standing up

- It has to be passive i.e. no internal batteries in the bass to boost your sound, or go flat at critical moments
- If it's active and it sounds really cool, ignore the previous rule
- It has to sound good in my headphone amp
- It has to sound good at home practice volume level
- It has to sound good at ridiculously loud gig volume level

Simples, really. Only I've yet to be able to tick all the above boxes with one bass, so my quest must go on. This is the bit I've really been dreading......this is a list of basses I've owned, and mostly sold on, that I can remember:

- Vox something or other, in natural - my first bass
- Washburn B2A active bass in red, with pointy headstock (it was the 80s) - my second bass

Then it all becomes a bit of a blur, so forget chronological order, best go alphabetical:

- Epiphone Flying V bass - what was I thinking?
- Fender Geddy Lee Jazz MIJ - fantastic neck, so so sound
- Fender Jazz AVRI '75 – natural, the keeper!!
- Fender Jazz USA - probably about six, either natural, black or even walnut (once)

- Fender Precision USA - probably about four, either black or sunburst, good and simple
- Fender Squire VM Jazz - one, can't remember if I liked it or not, I guess not, as I sold it
- Gibson SG bass - uuurgh, sounded like a dead fish being slapped on a fishmonger's block
- Gibson Thunderbird - four, loved them, hated the massive case and their fragile head stocks
- Hohner The Jack - headless, but cool-ish
- Hohner B2 - headless, not cool - the cricket bat!!
- Lakland Skyline Darryl Jones signature - s'okay, still went though
- Musicman Bongo - two, burgundy and stealth, impressive, but not in my hands
- Musicman Sterling - two, not impressed
- Musicman Stingray - two, one black with 2EQ (good) and one sunburst with 3EQ (not so good)
- Rickenbacker 4003 – five? Always black, apart from the Fireglo one, and the walnut one, loved the look, didn't like the amplified sound
- Rickenbacker 4004 - just the one, really didn't like it
- Sadowsky NYC Deluxe Jazz - fabulous, but far too nice for where I gig
- Sandbergs - three, maybe four, steady and well built
- Spector Euro LX Dug Wimbish signature - Churchillian, as in the dog that says "Oh, yes!"
- Squire Precision bass - cheap and nasty, perfect backup bass, doorstop, paperweight, whatever

- Status - four, including a Kingbass. Far too clattery acoustically
- Traveller bass - just weird, came with a free stethoscope instead of headphones (eh?)
- Warwick Corvette - one, top horn was too phallic
- Warwick Dolphin - two, wonderful basses but very fugly
- Warwick Doublebuck - one, too many switches
- Warwick FNA - one, far too light
- Warwick Thumb - three, maybe four, didn't warm to the sound, but did keep trying, obvs

I was once asked at a rehearsal how often I changed the strings on my bass. The guitarist interjected with "Never, he just changes the guitar". Looking at that list above, he may have had a point. Most were bought second hand and sold on for pretty much what I paid for them. I'd recommend this approach to all. The few new ones I've bought were sold at a loss, and I don't recommend this approach. New is fine if you can afford it, and you're sure that it's a keeper but I mainly stick to the second-hand market. I can recommend the Basschat (see their chapter) forum marketplace to all as a nice, safe and secure place to shop and swap. Hell, we're all at it on there, most of the time.

So, what am I currently using? Here goes, and why:

- Squire Precision bass in black, cost £50. This is the spare I chuck in the back of a car, and behind my rig at a gig, and is my just in case bass. If it gets damaged or stolen, I really don't care.

- Musicman Stingray 2EQ in black, cost £900. Sounds great with a plectrum, only I just play fingerstyle nowadays. I was playing it at the first gig my wife came to, so I'm not allowed to sell it, ever. It lives in its case in a cupboard, and rarely comes out.

- Fender AVRI American Vintage '75 Jazz in natural, cost £900. Looks fantastic and has that authentic vintage thump.

- Spector Euro LX Dug Wimbish signature, cost £1,800. Looks like the dog's danglies and, despite being active, sounds awesome. However, there was a fault with the pre-amp so it went back for repair under warranty. Then came the Coronavirus lockdown. It's currently at the dealers, waiting to go to the distributors, but it's actually going nowhere until this lockdown is over.

- Gibson Thunderbird in tobacco burst, cost £700. Look, I know I've had a few, and the case is massive, and the headstock fragility is still a concern......but they do look as cool AF, and I have a gap until the Spector gets repaired and returned, and anyways it was a bargain, and I will sell it on, promise. Update – it has gone, and is soon to be replaced by a Fender American Standard Precision. It was, and that is now up for sale, as there's now a Spector Euro LE4 1977 to pay for. Here we go again……

What have I learned from my roll call above? Only that I am evidently fickle, faithless, flighty and foolish (but not bad with alliteration, eh?). If I didn't gel with the first Rickenbacker, why buy four more? you ask. One answer is that all guitars are subtly different from one another, even if they are the same make, model and spec. Another answer is that sometimes for certain bands, a look or sound is required that fits and is right. The main answer is "Dunno, I just like buying them, but can't afford to keep them all, and one day I will find 'the one' that does it all" so until that day…….!

It's worth a quick word about luthiers at this point, and the best word to use is 'magicians'. If you're confident enough to do your own tweaks and adjustments, feel free. I never was and have always left it to the experts. I've had many a bass (see the list, I'm really not joking) with an action so high you could almost limbo dance under it, that a trusty local luthier has worked wonders with and transformed into something that's easy and a joy to play. I still sold them on, obviously, but that's different.

A setup by a decent luthier costs £30-£50 and is worth every penny. I had one brand new Rickenbacker bass with a dreadful action (it's not that unusual, sadly) that a top-notch luthier took care of, as well as some other work including replacing the bridge for one that actually works, and replacing 'that' pickup cover for a sensible bezel with thumb rest. It was to be his last Rickenbacker bass. He didn't die, he just said that he was never touching one again, as they were the proverbial bloody nightmare to work on.

[CHAPTER 30] – BASS AMPS

Oh good, it's time for another name 'em and shame 'em (or shame me) list, as I detail what's been used to make my sound bigger over the years. Here we go again chronologically, until I have to give up:

- A little 10-watt home practice combo was my first amp. This is compulsory for all beginners
- Traynor 100-watt valve amp and an H&H 4x12 cab aka The Wall Of Death
- Laney 100-watt combo - couldn't hear it, or feel it
- Vox 100-watt combo - heard it, felt it, didn't like it
- Trace Elliot BLX130 combo - punchy, complete with slot in front of speaker for parking bikes

Given up already, alphabetical it is:

- Ampeg Portaflex amp and matching cabs - looked cool, didn't sound that cool
- Ampeg SVT3 amp and 6x10 cab - great amp but oh, the weight of that cab
- Ashdown, various amps and cabs - never felt like they were all that
- Barefaced 2x12 cab - wasn't convinced
- Bergantino B|Amp and CN212 cab – a great pairing, and was almost a keeper
- Genz Benz Shuttle - okay, but more LEDs than a plane's cockpit
- Marshall VBA400 valve amp and 4x12 cab - loved them, but my spine didn't
- Marshall transistor bass amps (various) - never quite gelled
- Mesa Boogie M-Pulse amp and Powerhouse cabs - very good, and very heavy, respectively
- Mesa Boogie Subway D800+ amp - lovely, almost another keeper
- Mesa Boogie Walkabout combo - never quite matched the hype, I thought
- Orange Bass Terror - too dirty by far
- Orange Bass Terror V2 – it has a clean switch, now you're talking, love it, a keeper
- Orange ADB200B valve amp and cabs - too heavy by far
- PJB BG100 The Cub combo - aka The Shoebox, great for home / small gigs, another keeper
- TC Electronic RH750 amp and matching cabs - didn't quite cut it for me, and fugly cabs too

The desire is that warm, ever so slightly dirty, valve sound projected so you can hear it behind you, feel it on the back of your calves, and know that it's also filling the room or hall in front of me. The reality of achieving this for quite a few years has meant hefty heads and even heftier cabs. If I had a roadie, it would be an Ampeg SVT 2 Pro all valve head and an Ampeg 8x10 cab every time. Tone and clout aplenty, and someone else will be lugging it around. Some of the above on the list may not have been sold had there been parking somewhat closer to home at the time.

However, with the advent of class D amps and Neo speakers, weight is not so much of an issue nowadays, and plenty of heft can be obtained with relatively lightweight gear. My current Orange Terror V2 amp and Bergantino CN212 cab (OCD dictates that it will be replaced by two new black Orange OBC112 cabs – synergy, innit?) achieves most of what I want, and is all I want to have to lug into a gig. If I really need more than 500 watts, there should be a house PA to tap into and if there isn't, tough. My spine and I have done enough weightlifting over the years, and we are now taking things a bit easier.

For those of you just setting out, bear in mind that our ears hear logarithmically, so if you want it twice as loud, it needs to be ten times as powerful. Also, to compete with guitarists in that tiny little pocket of the audio spectrum they leave for us, bass needs ten times the power of your guitarist's rig. In essence:

100-watt bass rig too quiet? Buy a 1,000-watt rig and have twice the power.
Can't hear yourself over the guitarist's 100-watt rig? Buy a 1,000-watt rig.

The bottom line is when you start gigging, push the boat out and get a rig capable of at least 500 watts, ideally more. That should keep you going for quite some time. Less is fine if you have a quiet guitarist (ha!), but if you do, please let the rest of us borrow them once in a while, as it would make a lovely change.

[CHAPTER 31] – ACCESSORIES

Straps - buy a long wide padded one, ideally leather, with 'grippy' inner fabric, such as suede. You can always shorten it, and the padding does help, especially if your bass is hefty. Thin straps can feel like Pamela Anderson's bra straps in that they are desperately trying to cut into your shoulders due to the heavy load.......I should imagine. The non-grippy inner fabric straps may look cool, but they slide around and a gig can turn into a two-hour wrestling match with your bass. You may find that your style of music and playing dictates the strap length:

Death metal or New Order tribute - guitar hangs as close to your ankles as possible
Rock - guitar must be directly in front of your crotch

Pop - guitar in front of stomach, and let the air get to your crotch
Jazz - guitar is worn at nipple height
Slap - guitar tucked in almost under your chin

You can always shorten a long strap and punch more holes in it, but you can't easily lengthen a short strap. You may also find that the guitar hanging position rises with age, and ultimately may have to sit on top of the stomach rather than in front of it, as it's too much of a reach.

I did once make the mistake of buying a black leather guitar strap with chrome studs, that looked like it had been rejected from a sadomasochistic dungeon, presumably for chafing offences. That was during my overtly macho phase, which lasted for about one week until I thought it was too much of a faff.

Straplocks - highly recommended to all. Guitars plummeting to the ground seldom ends well, or cheaply. Schallers are okay but they sometimes work loose at the strap fitting end (coating them with nail varnish when first fitted tightly to the strap does help, and gives you a legitimate excuse for the nail varnish in your single man bathroom). You can do a fudge with Grolsch beer bottle cap inserts that is cheap (search on YouTube) and gives you an excuse to buy bottled beer whether you need it or not. I personally prefer Dunlops even with the challenge of fitting the 'where the fuck did that go' circlip. Once they are on, they stay on. (Just remember that when you sell your bass you'll need to put the original strap buttons back on, or you'll forever be buying yet more straplock buttons, just like me)

Guitar stands - try and avoid the flimsy ones that look like a converted Blue Peter Christmas candle mobile covered in black foam. The sturdier the better, and my personal preference is for the ones by Hercules with the Autograb mechanism. They can even cope with a Gibson Thunderbird, and that's a real challenge.

Leads - buy the best you can, and two of what you need. Some guitar leads even come with a silent switching mechanism that avoids the snap, crackle and pop when you switch guitars and have forgotten to mute the amp. These noises generally alarm the audience, may harm your speakers but will certainly scare small children and invariably make you look like a knob. For amp to speaker connections, it's Speakons if you can, and high-quality speaker leads (not guitar leads, ever) if you can't.

Plectrums - find the size and style that suits you, after all they are cheap enough. Brighter colours are better, as they are easier to spot on the pub carpet when you drop them. They will also turn up in washing machines, tumble driers and laundry baskets amongst other places. If you're prone to having affairs, keep changing your plectrum make, colour and size. The trail of distinctive purple Dunlop 0.71mm Tortex plectrums will lead your partner straight to the scene of your indiscretion.

Effects Pedals – it's possible to buy a lot of these and spend a lot of time arranging and rearranging them for the best err, effect, and ultimately disappear up your own backside when a problem occurs. I know, I did. My board randomly developed a fault at gigs whereby there was no output, then shortly afterwards all was well. How do you recreate that at home? Play for two hours and watch intently? Change every cable? Bypass every other pedal? Nope, sell the lot and buy a decent all in one multi-effects unit was my solution, and I couldn't be happier. Line 6 Helix FX unit, to be precise. Everything I could ever need is inside that unit, and more. I only recently discovered a pitch change facility so when a singer wants a song I know in E to be played in G, I just dial up the pitch change accordingly, and play it as I always have.

Tuners - buy one and use it. The headstock clip-on tuners work very well and are cheap enough. Keep a spare battery handy (generally a CR2032 coin battery) or even a second clip-on tuner. If it struggles with the bottom E, fret an A on the E string, or even the twelfth fret octave E, and it should then be okay, so long as your intonation isn't too wildly out.

Wireless systems - terrifically liberating, but they do need to be managed. If you have to select the channel it operates on, be ready and able to switch quickly to another channel if ever there is a clash with another wireless system user. It happened once to me at a rehearsal with our own guitarist, and can be a pig to switch both the sender unit and the receiver unit if you don't have the manual handy - typically we were both on the default channel, and both coming out of our own and each other's rig. Not good. Also, if your transmitter uses a 9V PP3 battery, just make a point of changing it after every second gig. You may get almost three gigs out of it, or even three and a half gigs, but you do look stupid when they go mid-song, so just avoid that pitfall if you can.

Many years ago, I had an early wireless system and decided to test it out for range at a village hall rehearsal. While playing I walked slowly backwards to the back of the hall, then through the doors, down the footpath, through the gate and about twenty feet down the quiet road. By then it was still working but acoustically weird, with the delay in striking the strings to when the sound eventually made its way back to my ears. It was even weirder when I turned around and found myself surrounded by a pack of confused local hooligans on their evening rounds. The strange man with the guitar in the middle of the road bid them

'Good evening' which seemed to baffle them further, and I calmly returned to the safety of the village hall.

Later that same evening my joy with my new toy was somewhat lessened when it picked up the CB radio from a passing minicab and transmitted it through my bass rig. Thereafter, and especially when gigging, I was always in fear of Car 67 and Driver 67 gate-crashing my gig, long after their one and only hit.

A lot of modern systems are now auto channel sensing, and have internal rechargeable battery packs, which takes care of most problems - just remember to get it fully charged before the gig. All things considered, it's much better to avoid the perils of a DIY bondage session with your own guitar lead at a gig, and you can walk out front for a soundcheck, and even go walkabout during the gig amongst the punters for additional coolness.

Batteries - always carry a few spare. They cost very little and can save the day (probably for other band members, who aren't as thorough as you are with battery management).

Rechargeable batteries - just avoid completely. A 'normal' battery will start to decay before it dies completely so you may get less sound from your active bass or pedal, but you should notice, and can then spring into action. A rechargeable battery doesn't decay. It's fine, and then it's dead. They don't save you money really, they just make you look like a bit of a dick when they go.

Cases and gigbags - if you can afford them, and your bass isn't an irregular shape like my Thunderbird, just get a Hiscox hard case or a Mono Vertigo gigbag, respectively. They are both the dog's danglies of their respective genres and offer better protection than an SAS regiment. You can stand on a Hiscox case should you wish to, and they are proven to be courier proof. When the dust settles after World War Three and only cockroaches are left alive to roam what's left of planet earth, I'm sure they'll be using Hiscox cases as their safe havens.

Earplugs – get some, the best you can afford, and use them. Remember, surgeons can fix most things nowadays such as hips, knees, hearts, etc. but they still can't fix ears. Simples.

[CHAPTER 32] – MUSIC SHOPS

Be nice to the people who work and run music shops, for they are our friends. They tolerate us as we fondle their wares and often buy nothing. They have to listen to endless slap bass solos, and numerous murdered versions of the guitar intros to Sweet Child O' Mine, Back In Black and Teen Spirit (okay, for the last one, the intro is the whole bloody song) to name but a few. They put up with some of us damaging their goods, and some of us even pinching the PP3 batteries from active basses (yup, really). They aren't well paid, and most of them are gigging musicians too, so late nights most Fridays and Saturdays. Yet, despite all this, they are still terrific people; humorous, knowledgeable and helpful to a fault. At no point do you ever get any pressure from them to buy anything, although that does occur naturally when you stumble across a gem.

Here's a few anecdotes from my music shop experiences....

When I lived in the West Midlands, a professional bass playing friend of mine and I would often spend Saturday's doing bass porn. This involved doing the rounds of PMT (the full name is Professional Music Technology - why is it known as PMT? BECAUSE IT JUST IS, OKAY?????), Guitar Guitar and Fair Deal Music, and sampling their current range of in stock basses. Said friend would pick up an item of bass exotica, and spend the next five minutes checking it out, via a masterclass of runs, slapping, doublestops, two handed tapping and lots more clever stuff up the dusty end of the neck. I did say professional. By this point we may have amassed a small audience, all impressed by his prowess. He'd often come to the conclusion that it was it was superb and offer it to me, for me to then have a go.

My thoughts: "You think I'm following that?"
My words: "No thanks, I don't like the colour."

Fair Deal Music used to have a cable on display next to a sign saying if you must play any of the following (Sweet Child, Smoke On The Water, House Of The Rising Sun, Eruption, et al), please use this cable. The cable had a guitar jack at one end and a 13 amp plug at the other. Top guys.

I was in Coda Music in Luton many years ago when Mr and Mrs Golightly entered, saying he needed to buy some more 'pleckums' for the guitar she'd got him for Christmas. Whilst the poor soul who copped for their custom showed them the various trays of 'pleckums' they had in stock, Mrs Golightly pointed at a whammy bar on a wall-mounted Strat and said loudly "See, that's where it goes, and that's not where you've stuck it". One can only begin to imagine where this guy's whammy bar had been inserted. The guy serving me said "My colleague often just hits them at this point"; probably a joke, but I knew where he was coming from.

A few years ago, I had to attend yet another dull as ditch water IT seminar in London on behalf of the company I worked for. Recent seminar attendees had started to dress in jeans and t-shirts and I nearly joined them that day but took a last-minute U-turn in the wardrobe and went suited and booted. When the seminar ended at 1pm and we woke up, we were supplied with food and were supposed to network with each other. Fat chance, what with Denmark Street and its music shops being just around the corner, so off I went and ended up in Vintage And Rare. I looked at a '62 Precision bass, price c. £9,500, that had been severely beaten to death over the years, and saw the sign 'Do not touch'. Let's get this straight, old damage is mojo and adds to the value, but modern 21st century damage will devalue it??

Anyways, they had three Jazz basses there, priced around the £2k mark, from the equally hallowed period known as the 70s that I was allowed to have a go on. This will be a blast, I thought. It wasn't; each one was a dog, sounded awful, weighed more than Gemma Collins and they all had necks like telegraph poles. I then reached for a cheap Squire Jazz bass and was stunned at just how good it was, and all for £200. Had I not been extremely poor at the time it would have been mine. I left there depressed and went to Tottenham Court tube station. The first train pulled in, I got on and was stunned to find myself stood in front of our Managing Director and one of his gophers.

Me: "I didn't know you too were in London today?"
MD: "Last minute meeting with a client. How was the seminar?"
Me: "Very inspirational and detailed. I'll send you my full notes later."

He'll never know just how close I was to being stood there dressed in jeans and a t-shirt with a guitar in my hand. Sliding doors indeed.

In the olden days, when I was young, I bought a bass combo from a small music shop in Aylesbury, and promptly took it back one week later after a rehearsal.

Shop manager: "What's wrong with it?"
Me: "We had a rehearsal and the problem is that I can't hear it."
Shop manager, thinking on his feet: "You're not supposed to hear bass, you're supposed to feel it."
Me, thinking on my feet too: "Well I can't feel it either."
Shop manager: "Okay, what do you want to swap it with?"
Me: "How about something I can both feel, and probably more importantly, actually hear?"

In fairness to the quiet Laney 100w combo, we did have a very noisy guitarist (no shit) but the Vox 100w combo I walked away with was at least audible.

Then there was the London music shop where the owner had moved on from a passive aggressive approach to requests he deemed stupid from customers, and now was just aggressive to almost all and sundry. So much so that the staff kept him in a workshop in the attic, well away from anyone, even though it was his name above the door. I guess we all have our limits.

[CHAPTER 33] – INSPIRATIONAL STUFF

I could not have let this book wrap up without putting a chapter together about the people, bands, songs, gigs, videos, movies and moments that still inspire me, or trigger a reaction, even now. This to my mind is the real power of music. Often it transports you to an exact moment in time that you treasure, or it will trigger all the emotions of that moment but without the detailed memory lane trip. Sometimes you have to think back to just why that song makes you feel so good, or even sad. Nevertheless, it's the music that triggers the feelings and emotions, and long may it remain that way. Here goes with what for me is going to be an emotional ride through my life. This could be tissue time, but for all the right reasons........

Songs

The Isley Brothers, Harvest For The World - this was playing on the radio as I drove home from the hospital just after the birth of my daughter Jodie, and shall forever be synonymous with that wonderful moment

The Rembrandts, I'll Be There For You – Not only the theme from Friends, but also the song that makes me think of Liam, my son. He'd probably prefer something like The Prodigy, and Smack My Bitch Up, but tough, my choice

Mike And The Mechanics, The Living Years - I can't help but think of my much loved, much missed and very dearly departed father when I hear this, and especially <u>that</u> verse

Bruno Mars, Marry You - fantastic song (cheesy video though, complete with dancing Jews??) that we liked so much, we had the musician at our wedding play it acoustically during the service

Van Morrison, Have I Told You Lately - our song

The Style Council, You're The Best Thing - our other song

Monty Python, The Bright Side Of Life - you can't listen to this and not smile. You just can't

Thin Lizzy, Rosalie - just pure unadulterated musical power, but with class. One band I was in always opened the second set with this song, 1 2 3 4 then cue the massive intro power chords, and we once nearly blew an unsuspecting punter off his feet as he wandered past us at this exact moment

Black Sabbath, Changes - when the heavy bands slow it down and go simple, they often produce pure gems, and this is one of them

Eddie And The Hot Rods, Do Anything You Wanna Do - oh Jeez, just so much energy wrapped up with catchieness (is that even a word? Computer say no, but I care not)

The Stranglers, Go Buddy Go - the first punk song that I really enjoyed

Rose Royce, Car Wash - the first time I heard a disco song and thought, some of it is pretty good

Odyssey, Back To My Roots - the first disco song I ever danced too (Perranporth holiday camp disco, 1980?), only the song was far better than my dancing

Pink Floyd, Comfortably Numb - oh, those guitar solos

Cheap Trick, Ain't That A Shame - the best song intro, ever

Status Quo, Backwater – another best song intro, ever

The Jam, Tube Station At Midnight - classic bass riff

The Jam, Happy Together and Ghosts - two gems from The Gift album that still make me happy

Steve Earle, Copperhead Road - catchy country rock perfection, and always went down well

Peter Gabriel and Kate Bush, Don't Give Up - I will get this bassline nailed, but it will never be as good as Tony Levin's on the record

Peter Gabriel, Solisbury Hill - takes me right back to my Sunday nights in with Anne Nightingale

Gonna Fly Now, The Theme From Rocky – stirring stuff to exercise too, when I used to, and particularly stirring when it’s used in the scene in Rocky 3 where he finally gets his shit together

Albums

Status Quo, Quo - let's overlook the latter half of their career and focus on their early stuff, and there's none better than this. Backwater, Slowtrain and Living On An Island really shows what they could do then

Thin Lizzy, Live and Dangerous - the best live album, ever

UFO, Strangers In The Night - the second best live album, ever

Cheap Trick, Live At The Budokan - third best live album, ever. Memorable for great playing, great tunes, and very high-pitched shrieking between the songs

Iron Maiden, Iron Maiden - their first breakthrough album, and what a pearler. Cracking songs and a gruff but appropriate singer, rather than the screamer who joined later

Pink Floyd, The Wall - a concept album, and still my favourite

The Jam, All Mod Cons - this saw off several styli on my stereo when I bought it. Angst, social comment, great songs, it's got the lot

Van Halen, Van Halen - superb rock songs, and they are all roughly only three minutes long, how does that work? Oh, and that Van Halen bloke could play the guitar a bit, too

Fleetwood Mac, Rumours - perfection, no more need be said

Bassists (some obvious, some not so)

Bruce Foxton, The Jam - constantly terrific gritty basslines and rather good backing vocals too

Phil Lynott, Thin Lizzy - 'nuff said

Adam Clayton, U2 - some fellow bassists get a bit sniffy about Mr Clayton's simplistic basslines. The thing is they are just so right for U2's songs. I'm sure the man who has entertained millions, sold millions and made millions isn't too troubled by them, and rightly so

John Taylor, Duran Duran - I once read two parallel interviews in a bass magazine, with John Taylor and Lemmy, and their answers were displayed side by side. Cutting to the quick, Lemmy knew every minute detail about his setup, whereas John Taylor just answered "Dunno, ask my roadie". Another pretty boy muppet who can't play, thought I. Then one day I had to learn the bassline for Rio, as the band at the time were going to cover it. My apologies, he really can play the bass rather well, and then some. My bad, entirely

Geezer Butler, Black Sabbath - rock solid rock bottom-ender, and none more so

Jean Jacques Burnel, The Stranglers - brought bass to the fore, with that dirty aggressive sound. His attitude helped, too. Legend has it he once saw a guy getting aggressive with a girl during a Stranglers gig. JJ stood on the guy's hand with one foot, booted him in the chops with the other foot, and never missed a beat

Guy Pratt, Pink Floyd, Madonna, Robert Palmer - never heard of him? He's well worth checking out, great player and pretty funny too

Movies / Videos

This Is Spinal Tap - but of course

Anvil! The Story Of Anvil – rather like Spinal Tap, only this is for real, and therefore both sadder and funnier

Africa (acoustic Toto cover), Mike Masse and Jeff Hall - search YouTube for Africa and pizza, it's top of the list. Just two musos playing in a pizza restaurant to not many people, but bleedin' superb. Check out their other stuff too

Moments

Common People - whenever us Common People gigged, we normally played the Pulp song Common People (obviously) towards the end of the night, and boy did we have that song totally fucking nailed. It just built and built and got better as it went. Bruce, our lead guitarist, would start leaping up and down like a crazy leapy up and downy thing towards the crescendo, every boost pedal was stomped on, and Russ would sing "I want to sleep with Common People like yoooooouuuuuuuu ooh ooh" while pointing at the audience. A series of purely magical moments to look back on, with that song.

During one rendition of said song at a gig, the organiser took it upon himself to start talking to me about how we only had five minutes left, while we were playing it. Not too challenging for me, as there's only three repetitive notes in the whole song (it's all about the feel, and timing, innit?). However, the staccato bit near the end was looming, so I said, "Hang on, complex bit coming up", played that bit perfectly as I recall, then said "Where were we?". Multi-tasking fail cleverly avoided.

Gunnrunner - we introduced Parisienne Walkways into the Gunnrunner set, and I loved it. Quite easy to play, but also quite easy to ruin with the wrong bass note. Steve, our singer / guitarist had the Gary Moore thing absolutely spot on and played it to perfection. I was always in fear of ruining his perfect rendition but never did, and the joy at the end of the song as the applause came in was always part pride, and part relief.

Intros - it still gives me a buzz when I play a song's intro on the bass, and it triggers a cheer from the audience as they recognise it, hopefully. The most popular ones I've done that illicit this response are Seven Nation Army, She Bangs The Drums, Peaches and Town Called Malice.

Freddie Mercury Tribute Concert - my youngest brother and I had been big Queen fans, him much more so than I. Following the death of Freddie Mercury, it was later announced that there would be a tribute gig at Wembley on Monday, April the 20th, 1992 and that tickets would be on sale soon. Fat chance of getting any of them, thought I. Only, one day through work I was driving past the stadium when Radio 2's Simon Bates announced that they had just gone on sale now. There followed the screech of brakes, my quickest ever bit of parking, some sprinting, and there I was, third in the queue at the Wembley Stadium ticket sales office. Two tickets purchased, and I was one happy bunny.

Come the very sunny day of the gig, we got to see pretty much a Who's Who of music. David Bowie,

Elton John, George Michael, Metallica, U2, Guns N' Roses, Def Leppard, Annie Lennox to name just some. Anyways, as night fell and it got dark, Queen and Elton John launched into Bohemian Rhapsody right up until the vocal multi-layered 'silhouette of a man' bit. For this the stage went black, and the original video footage was played on the big screens beside the stage. The next bit was 'the moment' for me.

The video stopped, and the band launched into the rock part towards the end of the song. The stage was suddenly and incredibly brightly illuminated, complete with umpteen thunderflashes going off, just as Axl Rose appeared in leather jacket and kilt, whirling around the stage in crazed fashion, and singing "So you think you can stone me and spit in my eye?" etc., through to the end of the song. The power and impact of that specific moment still makes my spine tingle and the hairs on the back of my neck stand up. Just breath-taking, and a once in a lifetime day, and moment.

Back to the humorous stuff. Having mentioned Simon Bates and Radio 2, it would not be right and proper if I didn't recount two of his classic on-air moments. His mid-morning radio show had a feature called Our Tune at 11am each weekday. This feature was made up of listeners' true experiences that they'd written in and shared, and almost always featured rejection, heartbreak, unrequited love, occasionally death and very rarely, a happy ending. Mr Bates booming yet dulcet tones would pour on the tragedy as he read out that day's story, and liberally lubricate the story with yet more heart wrenching words, generously applied with a builder's trowel. The culmination of the story was the playing of Our Tune, that particular poor letter writer's nominated song that encapsulated their emotions and said what they couldn't, or just reminded them of their loss.

So far so good, eh? Only, twice while I was listening it went spectacularly wrong, and then some.

The first moment was a tale of two hotel workers who met, fell in love, split up and left one of them pining for the other, and intending to use the Elvis song Heartbreak Hotel to convey their feelings. "Well since my baby left me..." would have done this perfectly, only Mr. Bates accidentally played another Elvis song, which was Hound Dog, instead. I'm pretty sure the pined for ex-partner was in no hurry to get back to her ex having heard "You ain't nothing but a hound dog" played live on national radio, just for her. Mr. Bates apologised, squirmed and then played the right song, almost certainly to no avail. Not after that.

Having read out another very sad tale of someone's recently deceased partner, it came to the moment where the song would be played, and this song was to be 'You're The Best Thing' by The Style Council. Appropriate enough, only Mr. Bates played it at 78rpm rather than 45rpm. Hence, the song went up about five tones, and Paul Weller sounded like Mickey Mouse as he started to sing "It could be discontent...." Oh, it could, and it was. The squeaky vocals had all the sombre properties of Joe Pasquale reading a funeral eulogy i.e. none whatsoever. The rpm was hastily adjusted, but the damage was done, and I heard it.

Parental pride – Both my children have been raised on gigs, guitars and trips to music shops, and I can clearly recommend this scholastic approach, based on the results I've got with them. Most parents are very proud of their children (Mr and Mrs Hitler being one possible exception), and none more so than me, especially when it spills over into my musical world.

At some point in his adolescence my son morphed into a clone of Justin Bieber at the height of his fame and popularity (Bieber's, not Liam's). As a responsible parent I thought we could cash in on this, and make a fortune, only he was having none of it, sadly. Still, I did have to smile at one gig where the drummer's daughter took a particular shine to his Bieberesque qualities, and constantly sat next to him in the pub while we played, even though he kept switching chairs and tables (and pubs, if he could). It had been many years since I'd last watched him play musical chairs, and this was almost like a flashback moment.

For me the defining moment was at The Feathers pub in Lichfield halfway through a Gunnrunner gig, with both my kids in attendance. Come the comfort and refreshment break after the first set, I sat down with them for a ten-minute breather. A lady sat nearby turned and said that she was really enjoying the music, and then looked at Jodie and Liam.

> Lady: "Are these your children?"
> Me: "Yes."
> Lady: "You do make extremely good-looking children."

I was never sure if that was a request to prove this point to her too, or if she had some link to either Mr Kipling's cakes or the child catcher from Chitty Chitty Bang Bang. Nonetheless, I still look back at this moment and smile with pride, irrespective of any potential missed opportunity to prove it to her.

[CHAPTER 34] – GLOSSARY

Here are some definitions of terms used in this book, and some other terms that I'd just like to get off my chest and define once and for all.

Auditions - a necessary ball ache, and occasionally enjoyable

Author - that's me now; also, a 1980s film with Dudley Moore and Liza Minelli, if you live in Somerset

Basschat – just the best website, like, ever

Bassists - the coolest, most intelligent and nicest people you'll ever meet. Humble, too!

Blues – a downbeat form of music mainly played by people who have befallen recent pet tragedies, often that very morning. If you're a dog, and your muso owner starts playing blues songs, get out of there sharpish

Cats – faithless shifty creatures

Children - awful things

Children (mine) - wonderful things

City - a place where you know nobody, as opposed to a town where you will know somebody, as opposed to a village where everybody knows everything about you, and often before you know it yourself

Cooking – sorcery

Cooks – sorcerers

Cooks who use stir-in sauces - saucerers?

DJs - people who'd like to be musicians but can't stop talking long enough to learn anything

Dogs – faithful but dumb

Drummers – terrific guys unless they're not, and then they're really really not

Drum solos - a break in a set where you can go to the bar and get a drink while someone who hangs around with musicians builds a shed

Fans - adoring followers of pro musos, and metal things that spin and keep amateur musos cool

Foldback monitor – something to trip over as you enter and leave the performance area

Food - an inconvenient necessity, as opposed to convenience food, which is a convenient inconvenient necessity

Fugly - none too pleasing to the eye

Gigs - places to get your kicks, that aren't necessarily on Route 66, and why we do what we do

Groupies - if only

Guitar case – a protective box for a guitar. Can also be used as a Trojan Horse for smuggling new guitars into the family home, undetected

Guitar solos - aural masturbatory sessions, why else the facial expressions?

Guitarists - very loud people

Kebab - the most dangerous thing known to mankind

Keyboard-ists – talented geeks with rhythm and big organs

Landlords – people with slurred speech who run small businesses

McDonalds - a very late-night meeting place for police, paramedics, post-gig musos and other emergency services workers

Metronome – a regulated clicky thing; also, a mythical creature that inhabits the French underground transport system

Microphone stand – a metal thing for keeping a singer's sole piece of owned music equipment off the ground

Minimum wage – an aspirational target for amateur musos, seldom achieved

Music shops - places that sell nice shiny things that hurt your credit rating

Music stands – metal things used by classical musicians who clearly can't remember things very well

My tone – the aural Holy Grail that musos spend many years and much money trying to nail and often end up just grateful that they can hear themselves. Also, a term of endearment should Martine McCutcheon ever land the female lead role in Anthony and Cleopatra

Rehearsals - as essential as air, and often just as interesting

Roadies - see 'groupies'

Set lists - a map showing the way from 1 2 1 2 to the encore

Sheet music – how a Mexican would describe most of the music that Simon Cowell is involved with

Singers - flaky egomaniacs who never ever own PAs

Sleep - see 'food'

Time signature – a way of describing 4/4 time; there are no others

Tuner - essential, also a type of fish for dyslexics

Wife – someone who knows more about the cost and number of guitars and amps that you've owned, than you do

Wives (plural) - to be avoided, more than one gets pricey and can be illegal, unless you're in The Osmonds

Women – baffling

1,2,1,2 – a sound engineer's PIN code

[CHAPTER 35] – ACKNOWLEDGEMENTS

This is the bit where I say more 'thanks' than Bill Clinton's Dry Cleaners ever did, or a first-time Oscar winner frequently does, and I'll also not be mentioning Harvey Weinstein either. How times change.

Here goes, from the top:

- Mum and Dad, for making me, without whom......etc.
- My kids Jodie and Liam, for letting me make them, and suffering a lifetime of gigs, rehearsals, music shop trips, motorway Basschat trade meets, and plectrums
- My wife Paula, for putting up with my nonsense, and getting me to write this book

Now, as you and I both tire, it's mainly namechecks only:

- Early days - Hippy, Snod, Druff, Dave, Gavin, Rob, Tony
- Mid-life (but no crisis) – Steve Noble, Russ Merrick, Steve Strain, Carrie-Anne, Jools, Mark
- Modern times – Russ, Dave, Clive, Bruce and Rob aka Common People, Leigh, Martin and JP aka The Rogues, Andrew and Pete aka MHTH
- Extras – pub and club staff, music shop staff, punters
- Book proof readers / helpers – Dave S, Pete M, Lyn H, Spike, Dave Holwill-Vader (Darth's half brother?)
- All the guys and girls on Basschat – you'll never know how much help, inspiration and humour you've provided me with over the years. Damn it, you're all such lovely people.....but stop selling me things!!!

If I've omitted anyone of significance then my apologies are offered, and it's entirely down to my age – I am getting on a bit.

[CHAPTER 36] – THE END WORD

I don't think the following bit belongs anywhere else in the book, so I'll just squeeze it in here – it's too good not to share.

My spritely eighty-something mother is a great source of inspiration to me. She's embraced the internet big time in the last decade, and is probably responsible for Facebook needing more storage, and half the world's spam, too. She emails, chats, Facetimes and shares more than anyone else I know, and is terrific, and not just for her age. She also occasionally mixes her words up.

Until today, the best one was "Don't let the jellyfish testicles sting you" but that has now been surpassed with a musical one hence it's inclusion, as follows: "Those kids singing This Is Me on Britain's Got Talent were so good, they got the Golden Shower". I really hope they didn't, for everyone's sake, not least theirs.

Before I go, just one final thing. If you've enjoyed this book, and I sincerely hope you have, please leave a review on Amazon and www.goodreads.com – it may just spur me on to do another book about my next 58 years of life 😊

Printed in Great Britain
by Amazon

51692533R00132